HALLOWED BE THY NAME

The Name-Glorifying Dispute in the Russian Orthodox Church
and on Mt. Athos, 1912-1914

HALLOWED BE THY NAME

The Name-Glorifying Dispute in the Russian Orthodox Church
and on Mt. Athos, 1912-1914

Tom Dykstra

OCABS PRESS
ST PAUL, MINNESOTA 55124
2013

HALLOWED BE THY NAME
The Name-Glorifying Dispute in the Russian Orthodox Church
and on Mt. Athos, 1912-1914

Copyright © 1988, 2013 by
Tom Dykstra

ISBN 1-60191-030-4

All rights reserved.

PRINTED IN THE UNITED STATES OF AMERICA

Hallowed Be Thy Name
The Name-Glorifying Dispute in the Russian Orthodox Church
and on Mt. Athos, 1912-1914

Copyright © 1988, 2013 by Tom Dykstra
All rights reserved.

ISBN 1-60191-030-4

Published by OCABS Press, St. Paul, Minnesota.
Printed in the United States of America.

On the cover: an icon of Antonii Bulatovich, written by Antonii Gunin. Currently located in the cathedral of the Holy Martyr Elizabeth in St. Petersburg.

Books are available through OCABS Press at special discounts for bulk purchases in the United States by academic institutions, churches, and other organizations. For more information please email OCABS Press at press@ocabs.org.

Abbreviations

Books of the Old Testament*

Gen	Genesis	Job	Job	Hab	Habakkuk
Ex	Exodus	Ps	Psalms	Zeph	Zephaniah
Lev	Leviticus	Prov	Proverbs	Hag	Haggai
Num	Numbers	Eccl	Ecclesiastes	Zech	Zechariah
Deut	Deuteronomy	Song	Song of Solomon	Mal	Malachi
Josh	Joshua	Is	Isaiah	Tob	Tobit
Judg	Judges	Jer	Jeremiah	Jdt	Judith
Ruth	Ruth	Lam	Lamentations	Wis	Wisdom
1 Sam	1 Samuel	Ezek	Ezekiel	Sir	Sirach (Ecclesiasticus)
2 Sam	2 Samuel	Dan	Daniel	Bar	Baruch
1 Kg	1 Kings	Hos	Hosea	1 Esd	1 Esdras
2 Kg	2 Kings	Joel	Joel	2 Esd	2 Esdras
1 Chr	1 Chronicles	Am	Amos	1 Macc	1 Maccabees
2 Chr	2 Chronicles	Ob	Obadiah	2 Macc	2 Maccabees
Ezra	Ezra	Jon	Jonah	3 Macc	3 Maccabees
Neh	Nehemiah	Mic	Micah	4 Macc	4 Maccabees
Esth	Esther	Nah	Nahum		

*Following the larger canon known as the Septuagint.

Books of the New Testament

Mt	Matthew	Eph	Ephesians	Heb	Hebrews
Mk	Mark	Phil	Philippians	Jas	James
Lk	Luke	Col	Colossians	1 Pet	1 Peter
Jn	John	1 Thess	1 Thessalonians	2 Pet	2 Peter
Acts	Acts	2 Thess	2 Thessalonians	1 Jn	1 John
Rom	Romans	1 Tim	1 Timothy	2 Jn	2 John
1 Cor	1 Corinthians	2 Tim	2 Timothy	3 Jn	3 John
2 Cor	2 Corinthians	Titus	Titus	Jude	Jude
Gal	Galatians	Philem	Philemon	Rev	Revelation

Books and Journals

EA	*Ekklēsiastikē Alētheia* (Church Truth), the journal of the Ecumenical Patriarchate.
IV	*Istoricheskii Vestnik* (Historical Messenger).

MO	*Missionerskoe Obozrenie* (Missionary Review).
MV	*Moskovskiia Vedomosti* (Moscow News).
NV	*Novoe Vremia* (New Time), a St. Petersburg newspaper.
OIB	*Ob imenakh Bozhiikh i imiabozhnikakh* (On the Names of God and the Name-divinizers) by Sergei Troitskii.
PG	*Patrologia Graeca*, Migne.
RI	*Russkii Inok* (Russian Monk).
RV	*Russkiia Vedomosti* (Russian News), a Moscow newspaper.
SD	*Sbornik dokumentov, otnosiashchikhsya k Afonskoi imiabozhnicheskoi smute* (A Collection of documents relating to the Athonite name-divinizing trouble).
SP	*Sviatoe Pravoslavie i imenobozhnicheskaia eres'* (Holy Orthodoxy and the name-divinizing heresy), by Abp. Antonii Khrapovitskii.
TsOV	*Tserkovno-Obshchestvennyi Vestnik* (Church-Social Messenger).
TsV	*Tserkovnye Vedomosti* (Church News), the journal of the Russian Holy Synod.

Contents

Preface	*xi*
Introduction	**13**
The Historical Setting	13
The Theological Background	15
1 A Book and its Critics	**23**
Na Gorakh Kavkaza by Schema-monk Ilarion	23
Ilarion's Focus on the Divine Name	24
Ilarion's Supporting Evidence	26
Ilarion's definition of "Name"	30
Ilarion's Warnings Against Possible Misunderstandings	30
Publication and Initial Success of Na Gorakh Kavkaza	34
Khrisanf's Critical Review	35
The Controversy Develops	41
2 Defender of the Faith or Heresiarch	**49**
Schema-Monk Antonii (Bulatovich)	49
A Theological Response to Khrisanf's Review	58
Retaliation Against the Author of Apologiia Very	73
3 Imiaslavtsy Victorious	**75**
The Ecumenical Patriarch Enters the Fray	75
Trouble Brews at St. Andrew's Skete	78
Ethnic Rivalries on Mt. Athos	82
A Melee at St. Andrew's Skete	90
St. Andrew's and St. Panteleimon's in the Hands of the Imiaslavtsy	94
4 Imiaslavtsy Under Siege	**97**
Retaliation Against St. Andrew's	97

Archbishop Antonii Gets Involved Again	*101*
The Ecumenical Patriarch Takes a Stand	*102*
5 The Russian Church's Decision	**109**
Debate in the Russian Press	*109*
The Russian Holy Synod Enters the Fray	*116*
Archbishop Antonii Khrapovitsky's Report	*120*
Archbishop Nikon Rozhdestvenskii's Report	*125*
Professor Sergei Troitskii's Report	*126*
6 Manu Militari	**133**
Archbishop Nikon's Trip to Athos	*133*
Nikon's Final Solution	*138*
The Deportation	*140*
Response to Nikon's Final Solution	*144*
Nikon's and Troitskii's Defense	*152*
7 The Pen Supplements the Sword	**157**
8 Truce	**183**
Debate Continues in Russia	*183*
The Athonite Monks Vindicated ... Sort Of	*191*
9 Name as Sacrament	**199**
A Sequel to Apologiia Very	*199*
Sergius Bulgakov's Contribution	*210*
Epilogue	**217**
Conclusion	**223**
Bibliography	**229**

Preface

This book is based on my master's thesis written at St. Vladimir's Orthodox Theological Seminary in 1988. Since that time, much has been written in Russian about the affair of the imiaslavtsy, but still little in English; and nothing in English tells the story as comprehensively as it is presented here. The historical and theological analysis you find in these pages remains accurate, and I have made few changes aside from adding to the bibliography some works that have been published since this text was written.

This year is the 100th anniversary of the most sensational events in this story, the expulsion of the Russian monks from Mount Athos. But the publication of this account is timely for other reasons as well. After lying dormant for decades, the theological controversy behind the tragic events that happened in the early twentieth century has re-ignited within the Eastern Orthodox Church. Church hierarchs can no longer command military forces to rout their theological opponents by means of fire hoses and bayonets, but the hostility expressed today over the Internet matches what was expressed earlier in ecclesiastical journals. One need only do an internet search for the keyword "name-worshiping" to find several web sites and web pages that decry in no uncertain terms the 100-year old "heresy." For that reason, the publication now of this account is especially appropriate because it puts a human face on the "heretics" and offers a sympathetic interpretation of the "heresy."

The dates of almost all of the sources are according to the Julian calendar, which during this period was 13 days behind the

Gregorian calendar. For example, when a Russian source records a date of January 1, 1913, according to our calendar the date was January 14, 1913. In general, I report the dates as they appear in the original sources. However, for some key events I include the new calendar equivalent for the convenience of those who want to correlate events of this story with what was going on in the rest of the world at the same time.

For help in the research and writing of this work I owe thanks to Fr. John Meyendorff, Richard Seltzer, John Dibs, Andre Orbeliani, Bill Bass, Stephen Beskid, Alexander Dvorkin, Edward Kasinec, Antoine Nivière, Hugh Olmstead, Johannes Remy, Mark Stokoe, and the library staff of the Centre d'Etudes Istina in Paris.

Introduction

The Historical Setting

On July 3/16, 1913 some four hundred monks of the Athonite monastery of St. Panteleimon fled to one of their dormitory buildings and set to work barricading the entrances with bed boards. Bayoneted rifles in hand, sailors of the Russian Imperial Navy surrounded the building while their officers exhorted the unarmed monks to give up peacefully. To no avail. Prepared for martyrdom but hoping in God's help, the monks sang, prayed, did prostrations, and took up icons and crosses to defend themselves. Finally the trumpet rang out with the command to "shoot," and the calm of the Holy Mountain was rent by the roar ... not of firearms, but of fire hoses. After an hour-long "cold shower" dampened the monks' spirits, the sailors rushed the building and began to drag recalcitrant devotees of the contemplative life out of the corridors.

These events took place on a narrow peninsula in northern Greece some forty miles long by five miles wide, named "Mt. Athos" after the 6,000 foot mountain towering over the end of it. Since the tenth century this stretch of land has been set aside for the exclusive use of Eastern Orthodox monks, a status instituted by the Byzantine Empire and maintained by the Turks after they conquered it in 1453. Though located in Greece it eventually became an international center for Orthodox monasticism, and the nineteenth century saw such a mass immigration of Russians that by the beginning of the twentieth the mountain was really more Russian than Greek. That situation was not to last long, and the events narrated above marked the beginning of the end. In 1913 the Russian government forcibly expelled more than eight hundred of its own citizens from Mt. Athos, and these were followed in succeeding months by as many as one thousand more who would have been expelled had they not left voluntarily.

Their crime: disagreeing with the Holy Synod of the Russian Orthodox Church in a controversy about the phrase "The name of God is God himself." The Synod's show of force was intended to end the debate and extort at least tacit agreement from its opponents – but it accomplished neither. Rather, it was but one of many turning points in a long theological dispute whose course was more often determined by politics and personal grudges than by theology. The history of this controversy is a fascinating one in its own right, but at the same time it provides insight into the inner workings of the Russian Orthodox Church. The practical value of that knowledge should not be underestimated – the Russian church at that time was no different from the other Orthodox churches, and the Orthodox churches of today do not operate any differently. Today's Orthodox hierarchs don't have armies at their command, but they and their willing minions often use what power they do possess in the same way as their predecessors described in these pages.

Besides that, this story is an excellent illustration of how the Eastern Orthodox Church has always resolved – or failed to resolve – its theological issues.

And last but not least, the debate reproduced herein can help clarify the Orthodox understanding of an issue fundamentally important for Christian theology.

The Theological Background

In the Old Testament the word we translate "name" (*shem*) is closely related to the one we translate "soul" (*nephesh*), and both mean something quite different from their common English usage. The ancient Hebrew "soul" is the essence of an animate being, not necessarily just of a human being; even animals are souls. You can therefore even speak of "dead souls." "Soul" designates the totality of the person. And so does "name," as an eminent Hebrew scholar explains:

> It is to be understood quite literally that the name is the soul ... the heritage consisting in the name is not an empty appellation, a sound, but the substance of a soul ... The name immediately calls forth the soul it designates; therefore there is such a deep significance in the very mention of a name (Pederson 1:245, 254, 256).

When the name mentioned and the soul called forth is God's, one is assured of divine action. "In every place where I cause my name to be remembered I will come to you and bless you" (Ex 20:24). "Whoever calls on the name of Yahweh shall be saved" (Joel 2:32). Therefore the divine name must be treated with great respect: "You shall not take the name of Yahweh your God in vain" (Ex 20:7, Deut 5:11). Blasphemy against the name is an extremely serious offense punishable by stoning (Lev 24:16). Even forgetting the name is a terrible sin: woe unto those "who think to make my people forget my name ... even as their fathers forgot my name for Baal" (Jer 23:27; see also Ps 44:20). And even the very mention of the names of other gods is to be avoided: "Make no mention of the names of other gods, nor let such be heard out of your mouth" (Ex 23:13; see also Josh 23:7, Hos 2:17).

The realism with which the name of God is conceived is often striking. The priests are to bless the people of Israel by "placing on them" God's name (Num 6:27). The name itself comes to execute judgment: "Behold, the name of Yahweh comes from afar, burning with his anger ..." (Is 30:27). It acts: "The name of the God of Jacob protect you!" (Ps 20:1). It is a place of refuge: "The name of Yahweh is a strong tower; the righteous man runs into it and is safe" (Prov 18:10; see also Zeph 3:12). It dwells in the tabernacle, later the temple, which is "the place which Yahweh will choose to make his name dwell there" (Deut 16:2; see also 12:11, 14:23, 16:6,11, 26:2, Is 18:7, Ps 74:7). The temple was in fact built specifically to be "a house for the name of Yahweh" (1 Kg 8:17; see also 3:2, 8:20, 27, 29).

Consequently, "to know the name of Yahweh" implies much more than knowledge of a particular combination of letters. Several psalms suggest that only the righteous know God's name (9:10, 91:14). And although Genesis 4:26 states that, "At that time men began to call upon the name of Yahweh," much later this very name is revealed to Moses as if it were not known before (Ex 3:13-15; cf. 6:2-3). Still later Isaiah promises that Israel will come to know God's name in the future, implying that it was still not known, or not fully known (Is 52:6).

The same theme continues in the New Testament, where Jesus says, "I have manifested your name to the men whom you gave me out of the world ... I have made known to them your name, and I will make it known ..." (John 17:6, 26) Here too, the implication is that the name is at once known and yet not known. Despite the entire Old Testament history, it is Jesus who reveals God's name (see also Rev 19:12-13).

What is especially remarkable in the New Testament, though, is that all of the wonderful attributes formerly ascribed to the divine name "Yahweh" come to be attributed to the name "Jesus." Its mention is an absolutely reliable assurance of divine action: "Whatever you ask the Father in my name, he will give you" (John 16:23; see also 14:13, 14; 16:24, 26). Not only does the believer find "life in his name" (John 20:31), but this life is not to be found anywhere else since "there is no other name under heaven given among men by which we must be saved" (Acts 4:12). Jesus' name is placed on an even footing with the Holy Spirit as the effective agent in baptism: "you were washed, you were sanctified, you were justified in the name of the Lord Jesus Christ and in the Spirit of our God" (1 Cor 6:11). And as did the name of Yahweh, this name itself acts: "And his name, by faith in his name, has made this man strong ..." (Acts 3:16). To suffer for the faith is to suffer "for the name" (Acts 5:41, 9:16, 15:26, 21:13), just as faith itself is "in the name" of Jesus Christ (John 3:18, Acts 3:16, 1 John 3:23). The honor due to this name cannot be overestimated: "Therefore God has highly exalted him and bestowed on him the name which is above every name, that at the name of Jesus every knee should bow ..." (Phil 2:9-10).

Hence, the name of Jesus has played a central role in Christian spirituality, particularly in prayer, from the beginning. And when monasticism arose in the fourth century with its devotion to literal fulfillment of all of the gospel's commandments, including those to "unceasing prayer" (1 Thess 5:17, Lk 18:1, Eph 6:18), that central role became even more prominent.

One way to make prayer "unceasing" was to persistently repeat a short formula, usually consisting of a simple cry for "help" or "mercy." Jesus' warning against "vain repetition" (Mt 6:7) was understood not to apply to repetition per se but rather to doing so "vainly." Indeed, he himself taught his disciples to repeat the "Our Father." But for many circumstances, something simpler than the Lord's Prayer was needed, something easily recited even while one was occupied by other tasks, yet expressing what needed to be expressed. Initially the formulas chosen varied from the ultimate in simplicity such as "Lord help" or "Lord have mercy" to somewhat longer variants such as Ps 70:1: "Make haste, O God, to deliver me!" But gradually one formula gained ascendancy. It was apparently influenced by the short cries for help people make to Jesus in the gospels, particularly that of a certain blind man who attains his healing precisely through persistence in repeating one phrase – "Jesus, Son of David, have mercy on me" (Luke 18:38; see also Mark 10:47, Matt 20:31).

Also of some influence was the parable of the Publican and the Pharisee, wherein Jesus praises the publican who prayed simply, "God, have mercy on me, a sinner" (Luke 18:13). The formula that became the standard by the thirteenth or fourteenth century contained elements of both of these with a few changes making Christian doctrine more explicit: "Lord Jesus Christ, Son of God, have mercy on me, a sinner" (sometimes without "a sinner"). It came to be known as the Jesus prayer.[1]

That title itself identifies the most vital element, the *sine qua non* of the prayer. Yet the other names "Lord," "Christ," and

---

[1] To my knowledge the best presentation of the historical and theological background to this prayer is Irenee Hausherr's *The Name of Jesus*. For briefer presentations oriented more toward practical aspects of its use and written by Eastern Orthodox authors, see Ware, *The Power of the Name* and Gillet, *The Jesus Prayer*.

"Son of God" were also of great importance in that they identified more precisely the "Jesus" addressed and at the same time made of the prayer a confession of faith. As for the nature of the prayer's request, the attitude of contrition it emphasized arose from, and was especially appropriate to, the monastic milieu – but at the same time it could also be understood in a wider sense. "Mercy" is sometimes taken to refer merely to the lessening of punishment due to an offender, but the Greek *eleein* (to have mercy) can also mean simply "to be good to" or "to be gracious to," particularly in a Christian context because of the way it is used in the Greek Old Testament. Hence, "have mercy" could be construed also as a request for "help" and "deliverance" – and ultimately for all that is included in the petitions of the Lord's Prayer.

So the Jesus prayer was both simple and comprehensive. It was at once a confession of faith and a request for all that one could ask for. And thanks to its simplicity one could use it constantly even while engaged in manual labor, as monks often are. The prayer eventually gained such general acceptance that it even found its way into the official rite of monastic tonsure, where it was and is commended to the new monk as a way of life. On the other hand, not only monastics could find this prayer useful, and with the publication in the eighteenth century of the *Philokalia*[2] and in the nineteenth of *The Way of a Pilgrim*,[3] the Jesus prayer

---

[2] A collection of writings of various church fathers from the fourth to the fourteenth centuries focusing on methods of monastic spirituality, preeminently the Jesus prayer.

[3] By now considered a classic even outside of Russia, this is the story of a person who wandered around the Russian countryside seeking to fulfill the

was on its way to becoming a nearly universal standard in Eastern Orthodox spirituality for monastics and non-monastics alike.

Over the years many Orthodox Christian writers advocated this formula and explained its usefulness in a variety of ways. Some pointed out that since anyone can say it anywhere and anytime, it makes possible truly unceasing prayer. Others noted that its simplicity facilitates shutting all other thoughts out of the mind save one – the thought of God. Some suggested that as a call for mercy it can help keep alive one's awareness of being a sinner in need of mercy and can thereby help to develop and maintain the publican's attitude which was so praised by the Lord. Many emphasized its saving significance as a confession of faith, recalling texts like St. Paul's "with the mouth is confessed unto salvation" (Rom 10:10).

And many stressed the vital importance of the divine name. The scriptural understanding of the power of Jesus' name was echoed in patristic writings throughout the history of the Christian Church, has directly influenced the very development of the Jesus prayer, and was explicitly referred to in numberless treatises written about that prayer. And yet one could always assert that some aspects of the divine name's significance could still be explored in more depth. Doing so might have to involve the use of phrases and expressions rarely seen before, but that would not necessarily imply the invention of a different belief or "dogma." One could reasonably argue that such new phrases and expressions simply clarify in a new way the same basic belief held

---

Apostle's command to "pray unceasingly" – and found the answer in the Jesus Prayer.

by all Christians from the beginning. This was the stand taken by one monk named Ilarion around the beginning of the twentieth century when he offered some new explanations of his own. His critics saw something sinister in his "new phrases," however. They felt he was not merely explaining what had always been implicit but was rather introducing something new and therefore false. The result was a theological controversy that degenerated to accusations of heresy, excommunications, fist-fights, "blockades" of monasteries, and attacks by armed soldiers upon unarmed monks. All due to one or two simple, but to some people scandalous, phrases.

1
A Book and its Critics

Na Gorakh Kavkaza by Schema-monk Ilarion

In 1947 an elderly monk sent this advice to his spiritual daughter:

> When you read the book *Na Gorakh Kavkaza* (In the Mountains of the Caucasus), omit from the middle of page *xi* to the middle of page *xvii*, as well as the third and fourth chapters. In those places mistakes have crept in. The enemy influenced the author in order to undermine the readers' confidence. Read it with trust, it is a very useful book. I often have a glance at it, for one can see that it was written not with the mind but with feeling and with the taste of the spiritual fruits of the one thing needful. (Father John 24)

This book he so ambivalently recommended was first published in 1907 and was intended to popularize the Jesus prayer. But it inspired controversy as well as piety. From the beginning, a debate about these "mistakes" arose, with one side considering them not to be mistakes at all while the other saw in them a heresy so vile the book was worthy only of burning.

The author was a septuagenarian monk of the great schema named Ilarion. He had received monastic tonsure on Mt. Athos at the Russian monastery of St. Panteleimon and had stayed there for more than two decades before departing for the Caucasus. There he lived first in the monastery of St. Simon the Canaanite and later in the wilderness in order to lead a solitary life devoted to prayer. Two more decades after leaving Athos he decided to write a book, the purpose of which was "to express all the need, importance, and necessity of practicing the Jesus prayer in the matter of eternal salvation for every person." (*X*)

The book was comprised of three parts, the first and longest consisting of a first-person fictional narrative in which the author presented himself as an anchorite traveling through remote areas of the Caucasus. In the story, this hermit meets another even more ancient and venerable starets (elder), and the latter deigns to share with the former some wisdom from his vast experience in the spiritual life. It is through the older and wiser man that Ilarion's own views are expressed. The second and third parts of the books are relatively unimportant, one being a summary of the gospels and the other a compilation of personal letters written by the author over the years.

While providing many opportunities to praise the natural beauties of the Caucasus and its unique suitability for monks seeking the eremitic life, this setting serves primarily as a framework for extolling the virtues of the Jesus prayer.

Ilarion's Focus on the Divine Name

Ilarion adduced all the standard arguments in favor of the Jesus prayer but placed special emphasis on the importance of a mystical identity between the divine name and the divine person:

> For the believer who loves the Lord and always prays to him, the name of the Lord Jesus Christ is as it were (*kak by*) he himself, our divine Savior. And this great truth is really sensed best of all when one practices the Jesus prayer of mind and heart. (*XVI*) In the practice of the Jesus prayer of mind and heart, done in a repentant attitude of soul and in deep contrition, with your heart's feeling you really hear and perceive that Jesus Christ's name is he himself our divine Savior Jesus Christ, and it is impossible to separate the

name from the person named. Rather, they merge into identity and interpenetrate one another and are one. (119)

Hence, "in God's name God himself is present – in his whole essence (*vsem svoim sushchestvom*) and in all his infinite characteristics." (11) Just as in Jesus Christ "the whole fullness of deity dwells bodily" (Col 2:9), so too "in his holy name abides that very fullness of divinity immutably." (118) Since it is "holy in itself" it imparts sanctity to us who pronounce it in prayer. Since it "contains in itself eternal life and heavenly blessedness" (263) it imparts those qualities to us.

Ilarion acknowledges that there are many divine names, all as fundamentally equal as are the persons of the Holy Trinity (*XIV*), but he emphasizes the name "Jesus Christ" because of the unique role of the Son of God as mankind's savior and because among all his names, this one alone refers directly to that role:

> The name "Jesus" means Savior, and he is so close to the human race, needed by it, and constitutes such exceptional necessity for it, that without him it is not even possible to think of our salvation. ... In all prayers rising from earth to heaven he is the Mediator, Intercessor, and Reconciler; only by him and through him do our prayers receive power and do we have access to the Heavenly Father and to the throne of grace. (VI)

Consequently our prayers should be directed first of all to him. And so "the name Jesus Christ constitutes the root and foundation, the center and internal power of the Gospel" (29), and on it depends "both our Christian faith and all of the church's worship and piety" (53).

Therefore the Jesus prayer, since it consists primarily of Jesus' name, can and should replace all other prayers in one's private prayer life. "It, excepting only the Divine Liturgy, with which nothing can compare, abundantly replaces any other practice of prayer of ours. Or rather, truer to say, it rests at the root and serves as the foundation of all our prayer activity." (260) One who is far advanced in the practice of prayer may even drop the petition "have mercy on me, a sinner" and recite just the names "Lord Jesus Christ, Son of God," or "Lord Jesus Christ," or "Jesus Christ," or even "Jesus" (though the final option is rarely mentioned and is not advocated). Of his own experience the author writes:

> With time and from long practice this prayer began to contract and finally stopped on the three words "Lord Jesus Christ." It became impossible to pronounce more than this; all was superfluous and somehow wouldn't fit into the system of internal feeling. But what an inexpressible, purely heavenly, sweet feeling in the heart, unattainable by any of the people of this world! These three Divine words as it were (*budto*) became incarnate, became clothed in divinity; in them vitally, essentially, and actively was heard the presence of the Lord himself, Jesus Christ. (324) For the sake of this [prayer] I decisively left every other spiritual exercise, whatever it might have been: reading and standing and prostrations and psalm singing. It constitutes my service both day and night. In whatever situation I find myself – walking, sitting, and lying – I only diligently try to carry in my heart the sweetest name of the Savior; even often just two words: "Jesus Christ". (325)

Ilarion's Supporting Evidence

Ilarion is not able to cite direct scriptural evidence for his assertions, but indirect evidence abounds. Those passages in which the power of Jesus' name is not specifically linked to the individual believer's faith are deemed particularly noteworthy, especially Matthew 7:21:

If this name is not God then why does it possess omnipotent power which produces great and glorious works, even independently of the holiness of life of those who pronounce it? This, by the way, can be seen from the words of the Lord, "many will say to me in that day: 'Did we not prophecy in your name and by your name cast out demons and by your name worked miracles?' And then I will tell them: 'I never knew you; depart from me all workers of iniquity.'" In these words is found a new proof, having all power of indisputable persuasiveness, that in the name of Jesus Christ, God's omnipotent power is present and therefore this very name is God himself (17).

Ilarion does concede that the name does not always give expected results, observing that in Acts 19 some unbelievers tried to use Jesus' name to cast out demons and got beat up for their efforts. Nevertheless, one can be sure that the name itself does possess miracle-working power when "pronounced with faith." (19)

As for patristic writings, St. Gregory of Sinai had said "prayer is God working all in all," so if St. Gregory "was not afraid to call prayer God" (45), neither would Ilarion be. Other statements, less directly applicable, could be found in other fathers from as far back as John Chrysostom: "Unceasingly abide in the name of the Lord Jesus, so that the Lord will absorb the heart, and the heart the Lord; and the two will be one." (*I*) Most are similar to this, the vast majority coming from later sources such as Kallistos and Ignatius Ksanthopoulos, Theofan the Recluse, and Ignatius Bryanchaninov.

The only authority cited who expresses himself exactly as does Fr. Ilarion is Fr. John Sergiev of Kronstadt (1829-1908), a man who although not having the authority of an officially canonized saint was nevertheless widely revered as one:

Let the name of the Lord, of the Mother of God, of an angel, or of a saint be for you in place of the Lord himself, the Mother of God, the angel, or the saint; let the closeness of your word to your heart be a pledge and a testimony of the closeness to your heart of the Lord himself, the Mother of God, the angel, or the saint. The name of the Lord is the Lord himself ... the name of the Mother of God is the Mother of God, the name of an angel is the angel, the name of a saint is the saint. How can this be? You are called, for example, N. If someone calls you by this name, you acknowledge yourself entirely (*vsego*) in it and answer; that means that you agree that your name is you yourself with [your] soul and body. (15-166, quoting 237-8)

Fr. John concludes that if this is true of earth-bound human beings, then it is so even more for God and his saints, whose ability to respond is not limited by a material body. "And so," he concludes, "the name of the all-powerful God is God himself – the Spirit everywhere present and undivided."

In addition to quoting authorities, Ilarion offers his own explanations. He observes that all Orthodox Christians acknowledge God's presence everywhere yet do not say it is the same everywhere: the divine presence in a church is not exactly as it is elsewhere; God's presence in the eucharistic elements is not exactly as it is in ordinary bread and wine; his presence in a believer is not exactly the same as it is in an unbeliever. How then could one argue against a special mode of divine presence in the divine name? (See *XIII*, 46, 113.)

Besides that, one must not try to apply logic where logic is out of place. Statements like Jesus' "he who eats my flesh and drinks my blood has eternal life" (John 6:54) and "if a person is not born again he cannot enter the kingdom of God" (John 3:3) are seen as similar in nature to Ilarion's own assertions:

A Book and its Critics

Of course, this must be understood spiritually, by a heart enlightened, and not by that fleshly reason which ... objects, "How can this man give his flesh to eat?" Or again objects in its complete misunderstanding of the matter, "how can a person, being old, enter a second time into [his] mother's womb and be born?" ... spiritual subjects are understood spiritually, in the light of their illumination by grace (11; see John 6:52 and 3:4).

Just as we do not fully understand the mystery of the eucharist and of baptism yet accept their reality, so we should approach the mystery of God's name.

As St. Paul writes, "The natural person cannot receive the things of the Spirit of God; they are foolish to him and he cannot know them, for they are discerned spiritually." (1 Cor 2:14) This spiritual discernment is possible only for those who have directly and personally experienced communion with God:

> Only such a person, due to the union of his heart with the Lord ... can without hesitation witness before the whole world that the name of the Lord Jesus Christ is He Himself, the Lord God; and that His name is not separable from His holy essence but is one with Him. He is convinced in this not by reasonings of the mind but by the feeling of his heart, which is imbued with the Lord's Spirit. Here one must apply the Apostle's words: "The one who believes in the Son of God has the witness within himself." (13; 1 John 5:10)

Ilarion uses words like "feeling" and "sense" (*chuvstvo* and *oshchushchenie*) to refer to a direct perception of spiritual reality comparable to the way our eyes see the light of the material world. So any attempt at explaining the fruits of prayer to one who has not personally tasted them is as doomed to failure as an attempt at explaining the sweetness of honey to one who has never tasted it or the variety of colors to one who is color-blind.

Ilarion's definition of "Name"

Precisely what then is this "name of God" through which one can taste the fruits of prayer? Ilarion stresses that it is never limited to particular combinations of spoken or written letters:

> Certainly one can also pray to the Son of God without the so-called Jesus prayer, even without words – just by a striving of the mind and heart. But firstly this is an achievement of those advanced in the spiritual life, absolutely unattainable for the majority; and secondly even in such contemplative, refined, and immaterial prayer the name of Jesus Christ cannot be excluded. Otherwise to what would the prayer adhere and to what would it attach itself? (76)

Here the very thought of God is equated with his name, and in fact Ilarion explicitly and frequently acknowledges "the Jesus prayer," "the name of God," and "remembrance of God" to be synonymous.[4] Accordingly Ilarion also acknowledges a sense in which all prayer truly is the Jesus prayer, since as one of the Holy Trinity and through his unique role as Mediator and Intercessor, Jesus Christ "constitutes its [i.e., any prayer's] internal power, even if his most holy name is not audible." (125)

Ilarion's Warnings Against Possible Misunderstandings

Na Gorakh Kavkaza does not present an oversimplified view of how prayer works. The book is full of warnings not to expect too much too soon; one must be prepared for years of hard labor with little or no apparent success. Moreover, prayer may even be

---

[4] As Pederson observes, such usage is typical of Hebrew thought as well: "The word memory or remembrance, *zekher*, is used in exactly the same manner as [the word name,] *shem*, in order to designate the name, and so also the soul." (1:256)

harmful if one does not attend to certain other matters, one of which is having faith in God. In a sense it is even impossible to conceive of prayer without faith; if one did not believe in God and trust that he listens to people, one would not attempt to speak to him. Consequently "faith enters into the understanding of prayer, as its essential part" (125) and is its "inner power and content" (74). Their relationship is mutually dependent: "Faith without prayer can have no movement forward, and prayer without faith has no effectiveness – is dead." (303)

No less important is humility. The spiritual life of movement toward union with God cannot even begin without a movement toward self:

> The movement toward self consists in a person's coming to know his fallen sinful condition and the corruption of all his powers; their complete incapability of good and constant tendency toward evil; and his extreme powerlessness in the matter of salvation. One must see all the inescapability and decisive need of God's help. This knowledge is higher and more valuable than any other knowledge because it opens to us the door to the reception of higher help. Without this knowledge the help will not come, and without that our salvation cannot take place. (193)

We must cooperate with that help by attempting to live according to the precepts of the gospel. But this requires first of all that we know them:

> The whole goal of our life and of all its content consists in loving the Lord God. But how can this be, when we don't know his deeds, his teaching, the qualities of his character, or his perfections (of course, insofar as this is attainable for us). For our part there can be no reasonable, correct relationship to our Savior without knowing his divine person. Therefore it is necessary to diligently study the earthly life of the Savior ... in all detail and in all

thoroughness; to delve into his divine teaching, to learn well his parables, and to contemplate his saving passion, death, and life-bearing resurrection. This is the only ground and living foundation where the saving tree can grow – the Jesus prayer. (301)

Ilarion suggests that the Gospel books actually be memorized. But then as we learn God's commandments we must try to abide by them, avoiding sin and loving God and neighbor, or else our prayers will be to no avail. For instance:

> If, due to our weakness and sinful habits or what's more by inattention and absent-mindedness, we offend one of our brothers, then it is absolutely necessary to use all possible means available to us to make peace with him and ask forgiveness ... this is the main thing in prayer. Without observing this you will have no success in prayer, even if you persist in it day and night for years. (50) If you retain bitterness against someone, then understand that your prayer is not acceptable before God but rather angers him. (196-7)

The author also warns that his advice about the Jesus prayer is not for just anyone but is specifically for members of the Holy Orthodox Church. Outside the church salvation is not to be found, and its rites are established by the Holy Spirit for our salvation and are not to be disdained. Indeed, it is that union with God given preeminently in the eucharist that prayer itself serves to establish and maintain.

It would seem that there are quite a few prerequisites to the practice of the Jesus prayer, but in fact they are not truly prerequisites at all:

> Those guides speak falsely, who teach one to acquire various virtues first; to expel passions from oneself, to purify the heart, and

then to begin the Jesus prayer. That's impossible. For by our own powers we definitely cannot do anything good, as holy scripture teaches us. Rather, specifically with the help of prayer, while practicing it, one must do all one's deeds. And this is appropriate to the true situation of our earthly life, that we in every matter ask for God's help. (264)

Even the ability to concentrate on the words of the prayer is not truly a prerequisite:

> Usually they say: "Is absent-minded, inattentive prayer, full of all possible [extraneous] thoughts, really pleasing to God?!" But one must know that it is not possible to do any work well immediately. Everyone knows this by experience – how much time, effort, and trouble it has cost each of us to learn the work he does in life. Just so, prayer, which is the highest science – heavenly, divine, holy, uniting us with our Creator – necessarily must pass through the initial stages of one's learning and getting accustomed to it, in a condition extremely weak, not corresponding to its great dignity. But this must not serve for us as a cause and pretense for leaving and despising it. (48)

The author laments that many, including some monks, are indeed neglecting the Jesus prayer, some of them even advising others against using it due to the danger of falling into *prelest'*. In the monastic milieu this is a technical term for a state of delusion, sometimes approaching insanity, wherein the monk mistakes truth for falsehood. While thinking himself to be serving God he is actually serving the devil; while thinking himself in the depths of humility he is actually in the heights of pride and vainglory. Monks in advanced stages of *prelest'* have been known to do things like jumping off of cliffs expecting God to save them. Ilarion agrees that practicing the Jesus prayer can lead to such a state but argues that this comes about only when no concomitant effort is made at maintaining an attitude of humility and living a sinless life, or when some method of practicing the prayer is made an end in itself rather than a means to the end of communion with God.

Publication and Initial Success of Na Gorakh Kavkaza

So to counter the trend away from the Jesus prayer *Na Gorakh Kavkaza* was written. And written well. Fr. John of Valaamo gave the book such a positive evaluation for good reason; it presents an authentic and accurate picture of Orthodox spirituality. As for what some would call "mistakes" and others "heresy," it is evident even in the text of the first edition that the author was well aware that some of his assertions were potentially controversial. He mentions that "for theological science almost everyone reproaches and condemns me" and that he learned of the inability of "fleshly reason" to accept talk of God's presence in his name only after asking many people what they thought of the idea and hearing the negative reactions.

Accordingly, before committing his opinions to print he took the precaution of writing to a large number of "authoritative and theologically educated" persons asking their comments. Most didn't bother responding, and those who did simply said they did not feel competent to answer his questions. Though satisfied then that his views were at least not obviously erroneous, he nevertheless expressed them guardedly. In *Na Gorakh Kavkaza* most occurrences of "the name of God is God himself" are qualified by "as it were" (*kak by*) or "for the believer" or a combination of the two. That such modifiers are found less frequently in sentences speaking of God's presence in his name may be a reflection of greater confidence in the defensibility of that assertion.

In any case the grand duchess Elizaveta Fedorovna (Tsar Nicholas's sister-in-law) saw no reason not to finance the publication of Ilarion's book through her convent of Sts. Martha and Mary; the ecclesiastical censor saw no reason not to approve it for publication; and a remarkably large number of the Russian public saw no reason not to buy it. Within three years its popularity even called forth a second edition – no small feat for a book of such content published by what would today be called a "vanity press." By 1912, subsidies were no longer needed, and the Kiev Pecherskaya Lavra reportedly paid Ilarion a large sum for the right to issue the third edition that year. However, commercial success is never a sure indication of universal approval, and in this case criticism was immediate and exceedingly harsh.

Khrisanf's Critical Review

Shortly after the first copies of *Na Gorakh Kavkaza* arrived on Athos in 1907, the monk Khrisanf of the skete of St. Elijah wrote a scathing "Review"[5] of Ilarion's book, hectographed copies of it, mailed one of them to the author, and disseminated the rest throughout the Russian communities of the Holy Mountain. One of his two main criticisms was against Ilarion's identification of God's name with his person:

> And so the author personalizes the nominal, immaterial "name Jesus" into the living and very highest Essence of God. Such a thought is ***pantheistic***, i.e. merging the essence of God with something located outside his essence. Such thoughts as Fr. Ilarion has expressed are not found in any writings of the holy fathers,

---

[5]References are to the version published later in *Russkii Inok* numbers 4, 5, and 6 of 1912.

and this is some kind of new teaching, fantastic and filled with vagueness and full of obscurity. See to what extremes conceit leads! (4:75)

Being "holy by itself" (*samo po sebe*) the name does sanctify us, but to "divinize" it (*obogotvoriat*) is a great error. Divine power comes directly from God himself, not from the name itself; we do glorify the latter and it is dear to us, but only because it serves as a means by which we can call upon God, only as a "mediating power" (*posredstvuiushchaia sila*). The process is similar with human names:

> [When] we think of some beloved person, then in our mind he himself is represented in his image and with his virtues, but not only in his name alone. His name only reminds us that it is specifically he and not someone else, and after all we love him not for his name but for his virtues or for a close relationship with him. (6:55)

Khrisanf adduces a series of patristic quotations saying that the goal of prayer is to establish in one's mind the thought or memory of God, and he warns against the grave dangers of "stopping only on his name alone." The true goal of all who pray is rather "pure prayer," a wordless – and therefore nameless – state of ecstasy consisting of direct communion with God himself. In that state "the name Jesus is without effect ... and a person doesn't even call to mind this name." (6:59)

Therefore to concentrate on God's name as Ilarion advises is to forget about God himself. This is why the fathers:

> ... created many prayers, in which everything relates to the Lord Jesus himself, as to the ***living*** One who gives us blessings, but not to his name. And in church services [one hears] constantly

pronounced magnification and glorification of the Lord himself and worship from us to him, but not to his name. (6:53)

Likewise, the martyrs suffered not for refusing "to deny the 'name Jesus'" but for refusing to deny the Christian faith.

Moreover, the logical consequences of Ilarion's views obviously do not come about:

> If the inanimate names in the Jesus prayer were incarnated into the very Essence of divinity, then they ***always*** and ***everywhere*** would have ***living*** and effective power ... However these names only have power in the prayer of pious people. (5:57)

Nor does even Matthew 7:21 with its suggestion that impious people were able to work miracles in the Lord's name support Ilarion's view. Rather, according to St. John Chrysostom that passage serves mainly to show that even those with faith to work miracles will not enter the kingdom of heaven without living a good life. And other fathers explain that the miracle-workers spoken to are false prophets who only pretended to use the Lord's name but actually performed their miracles by the power of Satan. Khrisanf himself thinks they may be people who once acquired the gift of working miracles but later "quenched the spirit." He interprets the passage as applying directly to Ilarion, for whom the words "I never knew you" will mean "You knew my name but not me myself." In any case, St. Chrysostom also explains that grace was given to unrighteous people to work miracles because God chose to do so in order to facilitate the spread of Christianity in its earliest days. "But now let Fr. Ilarion point to anyone from the unworthy [people] who produces miracles" (5:59). Presumably he cannot, and that disproves his teaching.

The other main criticism is that Ilarion ascribes disproportionate significance to the name "Jesus," advocating its use alone in place of the whole Jesus prayer. But in fact, avers Khrisanf, the other names are even more important, particularly "Son of God," since it "designates the divine Hypostasis[6] of the Savior and belongs to him before the ages, [before] all that was created by God, whereas the name Jesus was given to the Son of God afterwards, at his incarnation on earth." (4:72) Besides not being eternal like the others, "Jesus" is not even a divine name but a human one:

> And is it possible to merge this human name with divinity, when the very human nature taken up by the Son of God may not be merged with his divine nature and it only unites in his one person, while whoever merges them – then this constitutes a terrible heresy according to the conclusion of the Ecumenical Council. So much more is it impermissible to merge the name Jesus, which applies to the human nature of the God-man, with his divine nature. To attribute that which is characteristic and proper only of the divine nature to that which does not have this nature – this is beyond foolishness and impiety! (6:59)

Ilarion's position is therefore tantamount to saying that in the one person of the Son of God there are two Gods – one his essence and the other his human name Jesus.

The scriptural evidence cited by Ilarion is attacked as having been misinterpreted. All those texts in which Jesus advises his followers to "ask the Father in my name" and where miracles are worked "in Jesus' name" refer not to the name *per se* but to the Son of God's role as mediator and intercessor. Even Phil 2:9

---

[6]"Hypostasis" is a technical term to designate a person of the Holy Trinity (Father, Son, or Holy Spirit).

A Book and its Critics

("God gave him a name above every name, that at the name of Jesus every knee shall bow") provides no support for Ilarion's views: the name "above every name" is actually not the "human name Jesus" but rather the name "Son of God" which refers to the Lord's divine nature. The verse means simply "God gave to Jesus the name Son of God" and ascribes no special honor to the name "Jesus."

With regard to both of his main criticisms the reviewer radically misrepresents Ilarion's views by ascribing to "name" a narrowness of meaning foreign to Ilarion. As has been seen, the latter used "the name of God" to mean not only mere combinations of letters but also all that is meant by phrases like "thought of God" and "memory of God," a usage in accord with that of Christian scripture. Khrisanf might have argued against "divinizing" also this wider conception of God's name, but he did not; instead, he actually spoke of it as the true goal of prayer for which the name was only a means.

And Ilarion did not advocate paying special attention to the name "Jesus" by itself: in *Na Gorakh Kavkaza* that name occurs alone exceedingly rarely, and then usually in references to other sources that had used it that way. Ilarion spoke of his own practice of contracting the Jesus prayer to "Lord Jesus Christ" after many years (and infrequently to "Jesus Christ"), but not once did he mention using "Jesus" by itself, let alone advocate it. Rather, what is striking about his book is that "Jesus Christ" is used consistently as if it were one indivisible name.

Besides such misrepresentations the review is remarkable for its sharp tone. Khrisanf exclaims "How he reinterprets everything to suit himself!" and "This is something abnormal!" He calls Ilarion's views "idle-minded thought," "idle-minded innovation," "absurdity," and "extreme audacity." Ilarion errs because he "is guided only by his own opinion" and is in an "abnormal spiritual and mental condition," and he expresses himself "peculiarly and senselessly" and "thoughtlessly."

The review's tendentiousness suggests ulterior motives in its composition, and it turns out that evidence for such motives does exist. Apparently Ilarion maintained some ties with Mt. Athos after leaving, and among those to whom he sent the first copies of his new book asking for comments was one Agafodor, an elderly monk in a powerful position among the leadership of St. Panteleimon's monastery. It was this Agafodor who sent the book on to Khrisanf suggesting he write a review, and who collaborated with him on it. As for why Agafodor disliked the book's author, the contemporary historian Kosvintsev gives background information:

> ... several years before in Russia a "mother Natalya" had become famous for her clairvoyance. When this "seer" lived in Petrograd, poor and millionaires, simple bourgeois and dignitaries in gold-embroidered uniforms all went to see her for "grace." Natalya "prophesied" to all in the name of the Mother of God, whom she supposedly saw constantly before her eyes. And then, when Natalya came to Jerusalem, one of the highest Russian monks of St. Panteleimon's Athonite monastery came there and asked from the "seer" prayers that he be granted grace. When Natalya was returning to Jerusalem, the ship on which she was sailing stopped near Athos, and the aforementioned monk with many other monks appeared on the ship and prostrated themselves before Natalya. But soon she was exposed by one of the Russian monk-hermits as fallen into *prelest'*. And from that time her aura of clairvoyance left her. (142)

In one of the letters printed in the third section of *Na Gorakh Kavkaza* Ilarion responds to a request for an opinion about

A Book and its Critics

Natalya (written before she was "exposed") and reproaches his correspondent for dishonoring the Mother of God by believing she would act in such a way. A sample of his comments:

> You, of course are guilty for having light-mindedly believed extreme absurdity, and by that you revealed not only the absence in you of spiritual reason but also that you are completely without the gift of discerning "spirits," i.e., the spirit of truth and the spirit of deception ... (311)

All of the names in this letter, even Natalya's, were replaced with "N." as was done in all of the personal letters printed in the book, but Agafodor undoubtedly found these words offensive – for it was he who had not only traveled to Jerusalem to venerate Natalya but had also gone to prostrate himself before her when her ship stopped at his monastery. Hence he sought to return Ilarion's compliments.[7]

The Controversy Develops

Whatever the underlying causes for Khrisanf's review, it incited open quarreling about the significance of God's name, particularly the name "Jesus," among the monks of Mt. Athos. The strife was worst at the skete of New Thebaide, a dependency

---

[7] One wonders why Ilarion sent his book to a monk whose response shows that they were not on the best of terms, and if he knew about Agafodor's dealings with Natalya. If so, the inclusion of that letter in his book and the sending of the book to him might have been prompted at least in part by a personal grudge similar to what prompted Khrisanf's review. It is highly irregular for a monk to permanently leave his monastery; Agafodor being in a position of authority at St. Panteleimon's, it could be that Ilarion had left after living there for 20 years due in part to bad feelings between them. These must remain only conjectures, however, for there is no evidence to support any of them.

of St. Panteleimon's, where the monk Aleksei Kireyevsky actively propagated the views expressed in the review. A typical episode:

> ... he visited one ascetic, a doer of the Jesus prayer, on his name day. The hermit treated him hospitably with what he could, and then while conversing with the hermit Fr. Aleksei began to speak about the Jesus prayer [and] about the book of Fr. Ilarion, and daringly expressed the following opinion: "Well, what is the name of Jesus, that Fr. Ilarion ascribes such importance to it in the Jesus prayer? ... a simple human personal name, just like other human names." These words vexed the pious monk, upset him, and he asked Fr. Aleksei to leave him and go away from his cell. (653)

Reliable details on the course of these early verbal quarrels are not to be found, but a general outline can be reconstructed. Because of Fr. Aleksei's making light of the name "Jesus," some monks began to view him as (and probably to call him overtly) a blasphemer and a heretic. Consequently some refused to receive his priestly blessings or to serve Divine Liturgies along with him. When both parties complained to Abbot Misail of St. Panteleimon's he took no action against Fr. Aleksei but did take disciplinary measures against those who were refusing to have anything to do with him. Some he deprived of the sacraments for periods of from one to three years, others who were priests he prohibited from officiating at services for similar lengths of time, and others he reassigned to less desirable jobs. Some were apparently even obliged to leave the skete altogether or left as a result of the other disciplinary measures. Fr. Misail was not necessarily taking sides in the developing controversy at that point, however; his actions were probably intended just to promote peace and harmony among the brotherhood. Perhaps he chose the course of action he did because Fr. Aleksei's offenses were in word only while the others' were in deed – but precisely because the peace-keeping measures did not include restraining

Fr. Aleksei from speaking his views freely, peace and harmony were not forthcoming.

That the quarreling was so difficult to stop was due in part to factors other than theology and personal grudges. Aleksei was a son of wealthy land-owners (said to be a nephew of the famous Kireyevsky slavophiles) and had attended the Moscow Theological Academy. The monk Theofan, a hermit who actively advocated Khrisanf's views much like Aleksei did, was a graduate of the Kazan Theological Academy. Khrisanf had a university education. In general their side in the dispute was taken by monks with higher educations, often from wealthy and privileged families — and consequently often holding positions of authority in the monastic communities — while their opponents were simple peasant sorts. So to some degree long-standing tensions between the two groups merely took on a new form in this debate. Since the "intelligentsia" tended to look down on those they called *lapotniki* and *muzhiki* (derogatory terms for peasants) and despised their opinions as worthless, real dialogue and understanding between the two groups was impossible.[8]

Economic factors may also have played a minor role. Since much of the income of Athonite monasteries came from donations of wealthy pilgrims, any improvement in the reputation of the Caucasus vis-a-vis Athos as a place where pilgrims could find holy startsy could cause the pocket-books of Athonite monasteries to suffer. And of course some residents of Athos might resent any relative lessening of the Holy Mountain's

---

[8]Later reports of political factors (peasant-monarchists vs. intelligentsia-democrat/socialists) and ethnic rivalries (Little-Russians vs. Great-Russians) seem to be entirely spurious.

unique reputation just for the sake of Athonite glory, entirely aside from financial considerations.

Nevertheless, the importance of these peripheral factors should not be exaggerated; the dispute was basically a theological one. It continued for several years, remaining limited primarily to personal quarrels among the monks of New Thebaide. When the second edition of *Na Gorakh Kavkaza* appeared in 1910 Ilarion included a response to Khrisanf's review, but this apparently had little effect on the course of a controversy which seemed to be on its way toward dying a natural death. Then in 1912 something did affect the course of the controversy and gave it a new lease on life: Khrisanf's review was finally published.

That event came about because Aleksei and Theofan happened to be friends of the powerful Russian archbishop Antonii Khrapovitsky (1864-1936). Abp. Antonii was born to a well-to-do family and rose through ecclesiastical ranks of authority remarkably quickly: he graduated from the St. Petersburg Theological Academy at age 21, was tonsured a monk at 22, became rector of the Moscow Academy at 27, of the Kazan Academy at 31, and was consecrated a bishop in 1900 at 37 years of age. By 1912 he was archbishop of Volynia and a member of the ruling Synod of the Russian Church. There he became so powerful that in 1912 subscriptions to the monastic journal *Russkii Inok* (Russian Monk), which he had established less than three years before, were made obligatory for all Russian monasteries.

Aleksei had become close to Abp. Antonii as a student at the Moscow Academy, Theofan met him at Kazan. The former wrote to him complaining about difficulties with his fellow monks at New Thebaide and sent along a copy of Khrisanf's review. Though Aleksei made no request that it be published in *Russkii Inok*, Abp. Antonii decided to do so – and suddenly a controversy that until then had been the subject of private discussion and argument in relatively limited circles was spread to every Russian monk who could read or knew someone who could. Monks who were scandalized by Aleksei's verbal belittling of the name "Jesus" suddenly saw those blasphemous and heretical views propounded by a powerful archbishop. Those inclined to speak like Fr. Aleksei but who had not before seen Khrisanf's review suddenly had more ammunition with which to provoke the simple and pious. And Abbot Misail of St. Panteleimon's monastery was emboldened or even made to feel duty-bound to use stronger disciplinary measures against those who were ostracizing Aleksei – which led only to their more widely propagating throughout the Holy Mountain tales of blasphemy, heresy, and repression at New Thebaide.

Khrisanf's review appeared in three consecutive February and March, 1912 issues of the bi-monthly journal. An introduction by the editor informed readers that:

> Bishop Antonii has affirmed that *it is necessary to print in Russkii Inok* the review or commentary about the book *Na Gorakh Kavkaza*, i.e., in other words the bishop recognizes the commentary of the Athonite about the book of Fr. Ilarion correct, and the book *Na Gorakh Kavkaza* incorrect and for monks *useless*. (4:70)

Shortly after its publication, Fr. Ilarion sent a defense of his position to Abp. Antonii, but the latter refused to print it for reasons he himself explained in a short "letter to the editor" printed in a May issue of his magazine:

> The author's defense is not at all substantial: he writes about the usefulness of the Jesus prayer, but this doesn't touch upon his

divinizing the name Jesus. He writes about the holiness of God's names, but this speaks against an exceptional power of the name Jesus ... The very name Jesus is not God, for J. Nave and Jesus the son of Sirach and High Priest Jesus the son of Josedek were also named Jesus.[9] Are they really also Gods? The author's communication that many who have read the criticism of his book have stopped using the Jesus prayer is either an invention (because people have always been using this prayer who have not shared the author's superstitions) or highly comforting – if those who united it with absurd superstition have stopped using it and consequently were using the prayer while in *prelest'*. (10:62-3)

The "anger" of Ilarion and his followers as seen in their treatment of Aleksei is adduced as evidence that they themselves are in *prelest'*.

That Ilarion did not defend a special "divinization" of the name "Jesus" in particular, much less as a combination of letters abstracted from all meaning, is not surprising – for that position was entirely a creation of Khrisanf's review. But Archbishop Antonii could not know this because he had not even read *Na Gorakh Kavkaza*. He had printed the review condemning that book in his journal; he had given the review his personal approval as being truthful and reliable; he had refused to print Ilarion's defense; and then he had printed this scathing reply in place of it – all without even reading the book. Only in October of 1912 did he finally do so.[10] After nine months of frequent and

---

[9]The Old Testament names rendered "Joshua" in English Bibles are spelled the same as "Jesus" in Russian Bibles, actually a more accurate rendering since they are the same name. The English Bibles suggest a difference in these names which does not really exist.

[10]By his own admission; see *Novoe Izheuchenie* 872, also Bulatovich, *Apologiia*, IX and Ivol'gin, *Ob Afonskom volnenii*.

virulent public condemnations, that process will have been largely a formality; not only was the archbishop's mind already made up, but to change his position would have been extremely embarrassing. He didn't.

2
Defender of the Faith or Heresiarch

Schema-Monk Antonii (Bulatovich)

The simple peasant-monks, often illiterate and in any case not writers, were at a loss for how to respond to these new attacks. So when word got around that at St. Andrew's skete lived a "litseyist" (university graduate) sharing their views, they went to enlist his help. Help quickly turned into leadership, and in the years to come this litseyist virtually single-handedly carried on the theological defense of the divinity of God's name.

Alexander Ksaver'evich Bulatovich (accent on the "o") was born on September 26, 1870 to a wealthy family of nobility, the son of a major-general in the Russian army. When his father died just three years later, the family moved to a large estate called Lutsykovka which his mother inherited and which was situated near Lebedin in the Khar'kov guberniya of the Ukraine. There he lived with his mother and two sisters until 1884 when they moved to Petersburg so he could begin preparatory work at the Alexandrovsky Litsey. That school was renowned as one of the most privileged educational institutions in Russia, with a liberal arts curriculum including law and foreign languages such as French, German, and English – all oriented towards producing high-level government officials and diplomats. Alexander passed through each year with honors and graduated near the head of his class in 1891.

Instead of going into government service as was expected, he chose to enter His Majesty's Leib-gvardiya (Life-guard) regiment of Hussars – one of the most aristocratic regiments in the Russian Army. Entry into it was made possible by family connections. Five years later he volunteered for a special Red Cross detachment of Russian medical personnel going to render humanitarian aid to Ethiopian soldiers who were at war with Italy. Cornet Bulatovich rendered especially important services to the mission because he had used a few months of preparation time to learn the Ethiopian language and could use his expertise with horses to serve as a courier riding camels across long and dangerous stretches of desert. In his travels with Ethiopian Emperor Menelik's forces he was the first European to see many regions of Africa, and upon his return to Russia he wrote a book entitled *Ot Entoto do Reki Baro* (From Entoto to the River Baro) about his unique experiences.

After just six months at home in which to write that book and see it published by order of his regimental headquarters, he returned on another mission to Ethiopia, this one for the purpose of establishing diplomatic relations between that nation and Russia. His travels into more unexplored regions resulted in a second book, *S Voyskami Menelika II* (With the Armies of Menelik II), this time published on his own resources. To the present day both of these works have remained of such value in the study of Ethiopian history and society that the Soviet Academy of Sciences republished them in 1971 and has produced a number of other books about their author and his work in the years since.

For his humanitarian and scholarly work and for service to his country, Bulatovich was personally thanked by Tsar Nicholas II, received the Medal of St. Anne third degree and of St. Stanislav second degree, and was promoted first to lieutenant and then to staff-captain (*shtabsrotmistr*). After a third trip to Ethiopia,

Defender of the Faith or Heresiarch

Bulatovich requested active duty in Manchuria, where Russia was at war with the Chinese Boxers. There he distinguished himself for his bravery – and for his independence: apparently against orders he rescued a French Catholic Missionary whose life was being threatened by the Boxers. For that he received from the French Government the Legion of Honor award. From his own government he received two more medals and a promotion to captain (*rotmistr*).

At the end of 1902 Alexander Bulatovich's career took another sharp turn when on December 14 he accepted monastic tonsure. It is difficult to say what prompted this sudden move, seemingly out of character with the rest of his career, but his sister Mary Orbeliani later recounted that he had always been particularly pious, even from early childhood:

> We all three shared the same room with our German nurse. ... Sasha's bed was behind a screen. The wall over his bed was covered with pictures of the holy scriptures, the holy virgin, [and] figures of saints. And in the evening when all others were in bed for sleep, and the candle of the nurse not more burning, we heard from behind the screen Sasha kneeling, and getting up and whispering prayers! (Letter of April 27, 1973)

In an interview she also recalled that there was a particular incident in Manchuria that seemed to weigh heavily on him after his return:

> I heard that when he was in Manchuria he went with his saber and had a fight with a Manchurian soldier. Then he killed him. And this soldier fell upon him, and all his blood covered his face. Then this made such an impression on him that I heard that several days he could not ... eat meat ... everything tasted [to] him [of] blood. Then he considered that he is ... [an] assassin, that he kills. This feeling came to him from it. He was at the war, he killed many

people, but he had not this f[eeling]; but here he had the feeling that he commits a terrible human crime. By killing. I heard so. Because his friend, whom I know, and whom I met in Poltava during the revolution, he told me that he asked him, "Now, how many people has this saber ... how many heads have you cut?" And he was so depressed. He turned around and he cried. I never saw him crying; but this [man] said that he cried. (Tape 4)

Whatever the immediate reasons for it, Alexander Bulatovich's decision to become the monk Antonii was one to which he remained faithful for the rest of his life.

The Petersburg monastery he entered, Nikiforovskoye Podvor'ye, had been established by Fr. John of Kronstadt, and Fr. John was to play a decisive role in personally guiding the new monk through the first years of his monastic life. It was he who advised Fr. Antonii to go on the journey which ended with the latter's settling on Mt. Athos.

During one of his trips to Ethiopia, Alexander had rescued a very small Ethiopian boy who had been mutilated by an enemy tribe and left for dead. After treating and taking care of him there and naming him Vaska, Alexander brought him home to Russia, baptized him into the Orthodox faith, taught him Russian, and saw to his upbringing and education. But other Russians, particularly the school-children young Vaska eventually had to associate with daily, were not so open-minded about Ethiopians or about those who had been mutilated as this one had, and in time they made his life an unhappy one. On Fr. John's advice Fr. Antonii resolved to return him to his homeland, which he did in 1907. Returning from his mission he stopped at Mt. Athos – and stayed. He settled in the skete of St. Andrew, where within three years he was granted the great schema and ordained first to the diaconate and then to the priesthood.

For the first four years of the growing controversy on Athos he took no part in it and hardly even knew of its existence, being so engrossed in the monastic life of prayer that he knew little of anything that was going on around him:

> ... I led a life highly secluded, silent, solitary; I was completely occupied by my asceticism (*podvig*) [and] never went outside the wall of the monastery. Not only did I not know either the persons or the affairs of other monasteries, I didn't even know many of the monks in my own monastery by name, holding myself completely apart from all affairs. Nor did I know what was happening anywhere in the world, for I read absolutely no journals or newspapers. (*Moia bor'ba*, 656)

His sister recalled:

> He told me after, that he wanted to kill[11] his flesh and slept in winter on a stone floor which gave him terrible arthritic pains. He told that he and others spent the nights in prayer in the Andreevskii Sobor [church] where they were bitten by bugs. (Letter dated June 14, 1973)

Though this sort of thing kept him out of monastic quarrels, he had become acquainted with *Na Gorakh Kavkaza* already. One of the persons to whom Agafodor sent a copy of that "harmful book written in the spirit of Farrar" was Abbot Jerome of St. Andrew's. According to Fr. Antonii, Fr. Jerome turned the book over to him asking for a written opinion. He obediently proceeded to read it. Years later he recounted the decision-

---

[11]"Mortify"; see Col 3:5.

making process, which he says occurred sometime around spring of 1909:

> ... I decided at first to write a letter to Fr. Ilarion, in which I protested against this expression "the name of the Lord Jesus Christ is the Lord Jesus Christ himself" – since for my mind, also somewhat poisoned by rationalism and lacking in fear and respect for the word and name of God, it seemed scandalous that in some way the name pronounced by my lips, thought by my mind, could be God himself. "Isn't such an assertion by Fr. Ilarion divinization of creation?" I thought to myself. ... But when I wrote this letter, then a certain special heaviness of heart fell upon me, and a certain endless emptiness, coldness, and darkness possessed my heart. ... I suffered, but didn't understand the reason for this suffering, and didn't suspect that it was due to my denying the divinity of the name of the Lord. Apparently I too was about to irreversibly renounce (*otstupit' ot*) the name of the Lord as had Khrisanf, Aleksei, Theofan, and the other intelligentsia and half-intelligentsia on Athos from Russia, if the prayers of my unforgotten spiritual father John of Kronstadt hadn't saved me. (*Moia bor'ba*, 658-9)

At one of his last meetings with Fr. John, the latter had personally handed him a copy of his book *Mysli Khristianina* (Thoughts of a Christian) "for guidance." Now as Antonii needed guidance he happened to see the book, and opening it:

> ... I saw before my eyes the following words: "When you say to yourself in your heart or pronounce the name of God, of the Lord, of the Holy Trinity, of the Lord of Sabaoth, or of the Lord Jesus Christ, then in this name you have the whole essence of the Lord: in it is his endless goodness, infinite wisdom, unapproachable light [etc.] ... That is why God's commandment so sternly forbids taking God's name in vain, i.e. because his name is he himself – one God in three persons, a simple essence, represented in one word and at the same time not contained, i.e. not limited, by it or

by anything that exists. The great names: Holy Trinity; or Father, Son and Holy Spirit; Word; and Holy Spirit; invoked with living, heartfelt faith and reverence, or imagined in the soul, are God himself and bring into our soul God himself in three persons." (p. 46) I was amazed, crossed myself, and, thanking God for granting understanding, immediately tore up my letter to Fr. Ilarion and burned it. And right away that inconsolable heaviness of heart that had burdened me after writing the letter went away, and I returned to my former spiritual condition. (*Moia bor'ba*, 659-60)

He returned the book to his abbot with nothing but high praise, and afterwards had little more to do either with it or the controversy that arose around it until the spring of 1912, after returning from a trip to Ethiopia to visit and bring the sacraments to Vaska.

When the articles in *Russkii Inok* appeared and were brought to Fr. Antonii's attention by some of the New Thebaide monks, he decided a rebuttal was in order and began by writing two short articles. One was copied locally and disseminated throughout Athos just as Khrisanf's review had been at first. The other was published, with Abbot Jerome's blessing, in the April issue of the skete's own journal. In addition, on behalf of the New Thebaide monks Fr. Antonii composed an "Open Letter to Archbishop Antonii" dated May 7, 1912 and sent it to him with a request that he print it in his journal to set the record straight.

Opening with the customary respectful titles with which one addresses an archbishop, the letter proceeded to ask that he admit to having erred:

Falling at your feet, we ask with humility that you hear out our explanation of the error into which the editors (*redaktsiia*) of *Russkii Inok* have fallen, having believed untrue information ... Only God is infallible, and we, knowing the humility of Russian hierarchs, to whom the self-important infallibility of Catholic popes is foreign, dare to hope that you too, your holiness, will grant a place in *Russkii Inok* to these our lines in which we defend ourselves against the slander raised against us [which has been] placed in *Russkii Inok* and thereby proclaimed to tens of thousands of its readers. (*Moia bor'ba*, 663-6)

The letter quotes Fr. John of Kronstadt at length, adding that it is in the very sense meant by him that Ilarion and those who agree with him understand the expressions in question:

> But neither Fr. John of Kronstadt nor any of us ... raises the name of God, i.e. letters and sounds, by essence to the level of divinity separately from God, and we do not venerate the name Jesus separately from God, as Aleksei Kireevskii and the monk Khrisanf reproach us for doing. Let us ask Fr. Aleksei Kireevskii: has he ever heard that any of the hermits pray, "Name Jesus have mercy on me"?

Though the letter's tone was generally not polemical, its conclusion could have been phrased more diplomatically:

> First take the log (disbelief and blasphemy) from your eye, and then you will see to remove the twig (imaginary name-worship) from the eye of your brother (Mt 7:5). [Signed] Monks of Athos.

The archbishop was infuriated. Instead of publishing the letter he published one of his own in response:

> On Athos the quarrels are continuing concerning the book of the fallen-into-*prelest'* schema-monk Ilarion, *Na Gorakh Kavkaza* – highly related to khlystism, which like a fire has now engulfed all of Russia. The essence of this khlystic *prelest'* consists in their calling some or other cunning and sensual peasant an incarnated Christ and some or other filthy old woman the Mother of God and worshiping them in place of God, after which they betray

themselves to carnal (*sval'nomu*) sin. This is the delusion into which Fr. Ilarion is directing his foolish followers, himself not realizing it, we hope.

Ilarion's views would help them because they need only name someone "Jesus" and the person would be a God. Abp. Antonii's strident tone is striking; not only is Ilarion simply labeled "fallen into *prelest*" but his teaching is called a "khlystic heresy about divine worship of names, i.e. sounds" and St. Paul's anathema against all who "preach another gospel" is applied to it.

Similarly virulent is an article by the monk Denasy of St. Panteleimon's monastery which directly follows the archbishop's letter. Denasy presents what is supposed to be a letter written by Ilarion himself in 1908 in which the latter admits that he himself created a new "dogma." An excerpt of that letter, reproduced here with Denasy's parenthetical remarks, reveals the tone of the whole article:

> The formulation (*polozhenie*) of the dogma made by us is important, unusual, extraordinary (what pomposity!), and in the way in which we have formulated it (like the Roman Popes, so inclined to think up and formulate new dogmas) is not found anywhere (thanks for the admission!) except only in John of Kronstadt ...

Other articles appeared in subsequent issues of *Russkii Inok*, including a response by Khrisanf to Antonii's April refutation of Khrisanf's review. Khrisanf argues that in passages where Jesus speaks of faith or prayer "in my name" he not only means simply "through me" or "through my help" – and so ascribes no special value to the name *per se* – but also he is referring to his divine name "Son of God," not the human name "Jesus."

Number 19 of that magazine printed an unsigned letter "from the Caucasus" accusing Fr. Ilarion of leading a dissolute life. Whether that was more than unfounded slander is impossible to say, but at least in one respect the author expressed what was probably a common feeling, i.e., that Ilarion's turns of phrase had not been heard before and for that reason alone are to be avoided:

> ... some hermits here also say that if Fr. Ilarion had been of a good life, and even then only after [his] death, if his relics were glorified by miracles and included in the host of the saints, only then would it be possible to believe him, since *his teaching is new*. ... People lived without Fr. Ilarion's book and were being saved, but now it's as if one can't get by without it; it's just the enemy making trouble and that's all. (58)

The attacks in *Russkii Inok* only worsened the quarreling, and in time two distinct camps came into being, each developing names for the other. Those siding with Khrisanf called their opponents *iisusane* (Jesusites), *iisusiki* (Jesusniks), or *imenopoklonniki* (name-worshipers), besides the derogatory terms for "peasant" already mentioned. The latter in turn called themselves "confessors of the name" and *imiaslavtsy* (name-glorifiers), while they called their opponents *imiabortsy* (name-fighters).

A Theological Response to Khrisanf's Review

Fr. Antonii Bulatovich soon decided to attempt a more substantial, systematic attempt at a literary defense, not of Ilarion's book, but rather of the very phrase "the name of God is God himself." The resulting 190 page book contained much material found for him by scores of other monks who, though relatively uneducated, were nevertheless very well read in scripture and church fathers. Initially only 75 hectographed copies of *Apologiia very vo Imia Bozhie i vo Imia Iisus* (An Apology of Faith in the Name of God and in the Name Jesus) were distributed around Athos, but the book later was published in Russia and became widely known as the foundational theological work in behalf of the imiaslavtsy.

In the book, Fr. Antonii observes that although the phrase in question is not to be found in scriptural, patristic, or liturgical texts, neither is anything which would contradict it. Moreover, nowhere can one find attacks like those of the imiabortsy against the honor and divine dignity of God's name; quite the contrary, all these sources unanimously and constantly speak in the most exalted terms of God's name. Khrisanf says church services praise God himself and not his name, but in fact the texts frequently speak of glorifying his name, pleasing his name, praising his name, worshiping his name, blessing his name, serving his name, and the like (see 157-72). And so not only do they explicitly contradict Khrisanf, they are also completely incompatible with his understanding of "name" which would limit it to a mere symbol of sound.

And scripture agrees with the liturgical texts. The Psalms, for example, are full of statements absolutely irreconcilable with Khrisanf's narrow view of "name," such as: "... how majestic is your name in all the earth" (8:1); "May the name of the God of Jacob exalt you" (20:1); "O magnify Yahweh with me and let us exalt his name together" (34:3); [The Lord says] "I will exalt him because he has known my name" (91:14); "Save me O God by your name and vindicate me by your power" (54:1); "I will give thanks to your name, Yahweh, for it is good" (54:6); "Our help is in the name of Yahweh" (124:8); and "God is known in Judah; his name is great in Israel" (76:1). Similar expressions, where "name" is impossible to interpret as nothing more than a mere combination of letters, abound throughout the Old Testament. In Ezekiel we find one of many explanations that God acts "for his name's sake":

> Therefore say to the house of Israel, "Thus says the Lord Yahweh, 'It is not for your sake, O house of Israel, that I am about to act, but for my holy name, which you have profaned among the nations where you went. And I will vindicate the holiness of my great name ... Then the nations will know that I am Yahweh,' declares the Lord Yahweh, 'when I prove myself holy among you in their sight.'" (36:22-3)

What all this shows is that "God's name" actually has a wide range of meanings. It is often used to mean the glory of God in the sense of his reputation among men, as in the text of Ezekiel quoted above. In that respect it ultimately means all that we know or can know about God. And since this begins with the entirety of the created world as a revelation of the Creator, all of creation proclaims – and praises – God's name:

> Praise Yahweh from the earth,
> Sea monsters and all deeps;
> Fire and hail, snow and clouds;
> Stormy wind, fulfilling his word;
> Mountains and all hills;
> Fruit trees and all cedars;
> Beasts and all cattle;
> Creeping things and winged fowl;
> Kings of the earth and all peoples;
> Princes and all judges of the earth;
> Both young men and maidens;
> Old men and children.
> Let them praise the name of Yahweh

For his name alone is exalted;
His glory is above earth and heaven. (Ps 148:7-13)

And insofar as God has also revealed himself through his prophets in the Old Testament scriptures, the scriptures in their entirety in a sense constitute one very long name of God. One significant passage confirming the validity of this wider understanding of what is meant by "God's name" is in Exodus where the Lord fulfills a promise to proclaim to Moses his name – and does so not by uttering a single word but by making a long descriptive statement:

> [The Lord said,] "Yahweh, Yahweh, God compassionate and gracious, slow to anger, and abounding in faithfulness and truth; who keeps faithfulness to thousands, who forgives iniquity, transgression and sin; yet he will by no means acquit [the guilty], visiting the iniquity of fathers on sons and on sons' sons unto the third and fourth generations." (34:6-7)

The whole of the Old Testament is thus dedicated to revealing God's name – i.e., who he is and what he is like – and so all of its content is his name, or in other words all is included in his name.

Given this wider understanding of name, the New Testament corollary is obvious. As we read in Hebrews, "God, after he spoke long ago to the fathers by the prophets in many measures and in many ways, in these last days has spoken to us in a Son, ... who is the radiance of his glory and the exact representation of his nature ..." (1:1-3) Elsewhere Jesus is called the "image of the unseen God" (Col 1:15; see also 2 Cor 4:4 and John 14:8-9). Therefore insofar as he is the perfect revelation of God, he is the perfect name of God. More precisely, he himself is the only true revelation of God, the only true name of God: "All things have been handed over to me by my Father, and no one knows the Son except the Father, nor does anyone know the Father except the Son and anyone to whom the Son desires to reveal [him]" (Mt 11:27).

It is precisely this interpretation equating "the name of God" with Jesus Christ that makes sense of many passages of both Old and New Testaments. Isaiah 30:27, for example ("Behold, the name of the Lord comes from afar"), is thus a prophecy of the coming of Christ. In John 12:28 Jesus' prayer "Father, glorify your name" which elicited the response "I have both glorified it and I will glorify it again" is a similar case:

> ... the Father as it were says thus: "I have already glorified my Son, who is my name, by a multitude of miracles which revealed his divinity and glorified my name among men, but I also will again reveal the divinity of Jesus by raising him from the dead, and having glorified my Son, will glorify my name." (29)

This interpretation is confirmed when Jesus just before the crucifixion says: "Father, the hour has come; glorify your Son, so that the Son may glorify you ..." (John 17:1)

Also directly parallel to statements like the Father's response in John 12:28 are several made by the Son, like the one in 17:26: "I have made known to them your name and I will make it known, that the love with which you loved me may be in them and I in them." As Fr. Antonii notes, here the very requirement for God's love, for Christ himself, to "be in" the believer is knowledge of God's name – which is ultimately knowledge of Christ himself.

After *Apologiia Very* was written Fr. Antonii also found patristic evidence affirming that "God's name" means Jesus Christ himself. St. Maximus the Confessor ascribes trinitarian significance to the Lord's Prayer: "For the name of the God and Father essentially subsisting is the only-begotten Son; and the kingdom of the God and Father essentially subsisting is the Holy Spirit" (PG 90:884). Hence, "hallowed be thy name" means "may we glorify the Son through our lives and deeds" and "thy kingdom come" means "may thy Holy Spirit come to us."

So the meaning of "God's name" is not limited to a mere symbol of sound but rather includes both that symbol and the fullness of knowledge about God which the symbol designates – and so "God's name" must ultimately be equated with Jesus Christ. Accordingly, patristic statements that the imiabortsy quote in order to denigrate the importance of God's name actually exalt it, such as St. Basil the Great's "The thought of God established in us by means of the memory is the installation (*vselenie*) in us of God himself." (54) This in fact does speak of God's name, for in its widest sense, God's name is our thought of, our understanding of, our knowledge of God; it is all that we know and can know about him.

Such an understanding of "name" then permits drawing parallels between the current controversy and the fourteenth century one about knowledge of God. At that time St. Gregory Palamas defended against Barlaam the Calabrian the proposition that knowledge of God consists of direct experience of God which is given to Christians both now and in the life to come. This experience of communion with God, or "deification," is nevertheless not absolute since the fundamental distinction between Creator and created remains. So God is at once truly knowable and yet unknowable, accessible and yet inaccessible. St. Gregory explained this duality by distinguishing God's "essence" from his "energies" (or "grace," "actions," "works," "deeds," "characteristics," etc.). Only Father, Son, and Holy

Spirit are God by essence; all creatures are called into being by his energies, maintained in existence by his energies, and share in his life through his energies. It is thus through the "energies" that the Christian knows the unknowable God and is "deified"; i.e., "becomes God" by grace, though not by essence.

The church councils which affirmed the Palamite teachings proclaimed that the light seen by the apostles at the Lord's Transfiguration on Mt. Tabor (Matt 17:1ff.) was one manifestation of this divine energy, so Fr. Antonii suggests that "just as the divine visible light is an action of divine light and is God himself, so too the mental light of truth is a verbal action of God and is God himself." (5) In this way God's name as knowledge of him is equated with his energies which are God himself insofar as they are inseparable from his essence. It is on this basis that Fr. Antonii dares to call his opponents heretics, for he claims that they agree with Barlaam in denying both the divinity of God's energies and the unity of those energies with God's essence.

Fr. Antonii takes care to stress that he does not claim the name is "adequate" to God; God is in no way limited by what we know or can know of him. There always remains something beyond our knowledge, something yet unknown. Nor does he identify the name with God's essence, which is another way of saying the same thing. Nor does he divinize creation, for:

> We do not divinize the conventional sounds and letters with which the divine truth and idea about God is expressed, for these letters and sounds are not the divine action of Divinity but an action of the human body; nevertheless we believe that even to these sounds and letters is attached (*prisushcha*) the grace of God for the sake of the divine name pronounced with them. (188)

It is rather the truth itself which is the content of God's name and is expressed by the "conventional sounds and letters" of that name which is God himself.

That divinely revealed truth is indeed inseparably connected to the letters which designate it, for to understand them when hearing or reading them, and to pronounce them as a confession of faith or in prayer is never a strictly human action but is made possible only through a reciprocal action of the Holy Spirit. According to Luke 24:45, it was Christ himself who "opened the apostles' minds to understand the scriptures." And 1 Cor 12:3 clearly asserts that divine help is necessary even for a simple confession of faith: "No one can say 'Jesus is Lord' except by the Holy Spirit"[12] (see also 1 John 4:2). Likewise, the same passage speaks of a variety of "gifts of the Spirit," such as words of wisdom, words of knowledge, prophecy, etc., and summarizes all with the words "One and the same Spirit works all these things ..." (1 Cor 12:11) So these outwardly human actions are also divine actions and in that sense God himself.

This is precisely how St. Gregory of Sinai's assertion that "Prayer is God working all in all" is to be understood. Since even the imiabortsy don't dare say he was mistaken:

> We can't resist exclaiming on this account in the Lord's words "You blind men, which is greater – the gift or the altar that sanctifies the gift?" (Mt 23:19) Is it not God's name in prayer that sanctifies the whole prayer?! If each word in prayer is recognized as having divine power as a verbal action of divinity, then much

---

[12] Fr. Antonii (5, *passim*) quotes Slavonic "No one can say 'Lord Jesus' ...," which places emphasis on mere pronunciation rather than confession of faith, but his interpretation did focus on the significance of the latter rather than the former.

more God himself is the name of God and the name of the Lord Jesus Christ in prayer! Is it possible to suppose that the request in the Jesus Prayer "have mercy on me" could be God, but the name "Lord Jesus Christ Son of God" is not God? (54-5)

And the words of prayer are indeed inseparable from prayer itself, as John of Kronstadt affirms:

> When praying it is necessary so to believe in the power of the words of prayer, that you do not separate the very words from the very deed expressed by them: it is necessary to believe that behind the word, as a shadow behind a body, follows also the deed, just as with the Lord word and deed are inseparable (qtd. in *Apologiia Very* 55).

This is what the Lord meant when he advised absolute confidence in the power of prayer, as in Mark 11:24: "... everything which you pray and ask for, believe that you have received it and it will be unto you." And so Fr. John explains that God himself is indeed present in every single word of prayer:

> God is a Spirit, a simple Essence, but how does a Spirit manifest itself? – in thought, word, and deed. Therefore God, as a simple Essence, does not consist of a series or a multitude of thoughts, or of a multitude of deeds or works, but rather he is wholly (*On ves'*) in one simple thought – **God-Trinity**, or in one simple word – **Trinity**, or in three persons united into one. But he himself is also in all that exists; he penetrates all [and] fills all with himself. For instance, you read a prayer, and he is wholly in each word, as a holy fire penetrating each word. Each person can experience this if one prays sincerely [and] fervently, with faith and love. But especially he is wholly in the names which belong to him: Father, Son, and Holy Spirit [etc.] ... (qtd. in *Apologiia Very*, 81).

In any case, God's name in prayer is not a mere means for calling upon him; it is not, as Khrisanf says, a "mediating power" (*posredstvuiushchaia sila*). No scriptural or patristic evidence for this assertion exists, and it is objectionable insofar as it suggests that the power of the name is not an active power, is secondary, or is not divine. The "mediating power" is in fact the individual's faith rather than God's name. Evidence for the divine name as the active power is found in Acts 3:16 ("His name has strengthened this man ...") and Matthew 18:20 ("For where two or three have gathered together in my name, there I am in their midst"). Here Fr. Antonii emphasizes that the Lord does not say "I will come" or "I will be there," but "there I am" – expressing an immediacy strongly suggestive of his presence in the name itself. Support for Fr. Antonii's view of the relationship between God's name and the individual's faith also comes from St. John Chrysostom, who writes that when people have not been healed by the invocation of the divine name, "this occurred due to their lack of faith, and not because of the powerlessness of the pronounced name; in just the same way many touched Jesus and pressed against him and received no benefit, but the woman with the flow of blood, having touched not [his] body but the edge of his clothing" was healed (60).

Therefore it is through the power of the name that the sacraments are performed. If they were made effective by the faith of the priest, then a faithless or absent-minded priest would be disastrous for his flock. And ascribing their effectiveness to the faith of individual believers constitutes Lutheran receptionism. Neither is true. God acts in the sacraments for the sake of his name. Invocation of the name is thus at the heart of every sacrament, and its use in prayer is similarly reliable: "We acknowledge the efficacy of every invocation of the name of God, either for salvation or for condemnation, for we believe that the name of God is God himself" (15).

Icons and crosses too are sanctified by the name imprinted on them, or rather their sanctification consists in their being forms of God's name:

> Are not the very lines of the face of the Lord on the icon a graphic depiction of the names of the characteristics of humility and mercifulness of Jesus? ... Is not also the sign of the cross a depiction of the name of the crucified Jesus, and is not its power borrowed from the name of Jesus? (170)

As for that very name Jesus, one of Khrisanf's worst mistakes was to ascribe it to the Lord's human nature only. It was the iconoclasts who argued that one could not make a true icon of Jesus because it would portray only his human nature. But that view was rejected by the church when it decided that the image depicts the person in his entirety. Since in Christ the two natures are inseparable, an image of Christ truly is an image not only of a human being but of God himself. Clearly, the same is true of the name Jesus, which therefore includes within itself all other names of the Son of God as well. Khrisanf's view thus essentially splits the Lord into two persons and is or leads to the heresy of nestorianism.[13]

The imiabortsy even go so far as to say that "Jesus" is not only not the name "above all names" but is actually the "least of all names," though the latter expression they have not ventured to put in print. They interpret all of the Lord's commandments to "ask" and "have faith" "in my name" as referring to "Son of God" rather than "Jesus," yet the Lord himself when he appeared

---

[13]The council of Ephesus in 431 condemned Nestorius for believing that the Son of God and the man Jesus were two distinct persons; it proclaimed instead that he was and is one person in two natures, i.e., one person both truly God and truly man.

to Paul – even after his earthly life – told him simply "I am Jesus." (Acts 9:5) As for their claim that the name "Jesus" is least important because it is the "youngest" of the Lord's names, in fact it is not relatively new but is as eternal as God's plan of salvation, which idea it expresses. In any case, all God's names are essentially equal in their divine dignity and power, all, as it were, rays of the one sun.

Yet for Christians, "Jesus" is indeed somehow special insofar as it is the personal name of Jesus Christ, the Son of God who is our Savior. It is that meaning and the Lord's fulfillment of that role that gives us particular confidence to pray to God:

> The name above all names is "Jesus" also because by the very sense expressed by it – Savior who has come to save sinners – it gives to sinners greater boldness in prayer to him above his other names. Actually – is it possible for a sinner to boldly dare to call God "Father" when he knows himself by his sins to be a child of the devil and a son of evil and of malice and a vessel of uncleanness!? Is it possible with a clean conscience to call God the Lord for one who knows himself to be enslaved to money, pride, and passions!? But look – even the most inveterate sinner can boldly and cleanheartedly call the Lord "Jesus," with hope and intrepid expectation of being forgiven and granted mercy, because the Lord so deigned to be named and to justify his name "Jesus – Savior of sinners" on the cross. (115-6)

In later works, Fr. Antonii also points out that St. Peter was specifically comparing the name "Jesus" to the Old Testament names of God when he proclaimed to the Jewish high priests that "... there is no other name under heaven that has been given among men by which we must be saved." (Acts 4:12)

Nor is the Son of God's name Jesus to be considered equal to that of humans who have borne the same name, as Abp. Antonii claims. For there is only one true Jesus; those in the Old Testament were foreshadowings of the one who was to come. Joshua (whose name in Greek is identical to that of Jesus) himself was an antitype of Jesus Christ insofar as God prophesied through Moses that an "angel," "in whom is my name," would lead the Israelites into the promised land (Ex 23:20-1) – and it was Joshua himself who led them there. In any case only Jesus Christ can perfectly justify that name's meaning "savior." And besides, the topic of discussion is after all not a mere combination of letters considered abstractly apart from all meaning but rather "Jesus" specifically as the personal name of the Son of God. And where in any Christian literature written anytime anywhere can be found attacks upon the dignity and importance of that name?

The end result of all these attacks on Jesus' name will be that monks will grow lax in their practice of the Jesus prayer. Some have even openly suggested that one need not think of Jesus' name in prayer, that the divine name in prayer is like the address on the envelope of a letter, while the prayer itself is like the letter itself, wherein the name need not even be mentioned. This is a teaching that will surely lead to *prelest'*, as Fr. Antonii explains:

> Every conversation of one person with another depends on a certain guiding thought which induces me to turn to that person and which compels me to say to him one thing and not another. It is not difficult to prove that this very guiding thought is a kind of name of the other person and is also a consciousness of certain of one's own personal qualities, i.e. a kind of name of oneself. Thus, for example, a person realizes he is sick and goes to a doctor; consequently, in order to turn to the doctor, what must the person at first think in his mind but two names: his own name – "sick" and the name of the other – "doctor." So the person comes to the doctor and believes in the name "doctor," that he is in actual fact a

doctor, and accordingly carries on a conversation with the doctor about his sickness, holding in his mind the whole time the two designations: I am "sick," and this man is "doctor." (48-9)

Here it becomes clear that by insisting on the name's importance in prayer Fr. Antonii is insisting on the importance of remembering the personal identity both of him to whom the prayer is addressed and of oneself. In prayer the necessary "guiding thought" is that prayer consists of interaction between a sinful human person and the personal God who is ready, willing, and able to help:

> In order to turn to God, the one who prays necessarily must imagine in his mind some designation of the characteristics of God, i.e. some name of God, as for instance: either "Good One" or "Awesome One" or "Great One" or "our Savior" or "our Creator" or "Sweetest Jesus" or "He who commanded to us to ask for everything from him and to believe in the fulfillment of the request" or "He who forbade under fear of eternal punishment that sin which I did." These are all designations or names of God held in the mind of the one praying, according to which he guides the words of prayer. Just so it is necessary for the person to hold in his consciousness also a certain designation of his own or a name, as for instance, that I am powerless, unhappy, or sinful, or that I have been blessed by God, or that I am a son of God by grace, or that I am dust and ashes. (50)

If one ceases to think of God as a real person (or rather one God in three persons) or forgets who he is, one is no longer speaking to the true God but a figment of one's imagination. Thinking to do without the name in prayer the imiabortsy are thus either truly in *prelest'* trying to imagine an unimaginable "essence" or do not understand what God's name truly is:

Is it even possible to think anything about God that would not at the same time be a depiction of his name? Are not all the nameable characteristics of God his name? Is not the remembrance of all the deeds of God contemplation of his characteristics? Are not contemplated in all the words of God his wisdom, goodness, and truth? No matter where you direct your eye – to scripture, to miracles, to his words or to his deeds – everywhere you will inevitably contemplate his name, and in the whole gospel and in the whole history of our redemption by God the Word you will read the name "Jesus" – "God the Redeemer". (54)

All of these arguments are authentic expressions of Orthodox Christianity, but the first-time reader of *Apologiia Very* will be struck by the polemical tone, the relatively poor organization, and the sometimes strained interpretations to make quotations seem more favorable to Fr. Antonii's thesis than they might in reality be. It is not difficult to see that one inclined to Khrisanf's view of God's name as merely a means for calling upon him in prayer would not be convinced by a multitude of references to miracles or healings worked "in the name" or "by the name."

In addition, Fr. Antonii could have been a bit more judicious in his choice of examples to support his position. Some seem bound rather to put off rather than to convince, such as one used to support the assertion that God's name (as opposed to the individual's faith) is the effective force in the sacraments:

> We recall a description in the Prologue for January 8 of how certain children thought of serving a Liturgy for a joke, and, having placed on a rock the bread of offering and the wine, and having read all the prescribed prayers ... they read also the words of changing – and fire fell from heaven and consumed both the sacrifice and the rock, and they fell down senseless. (15)

Nevertheless, considering that *Apologiia Very* is the work of one who did not have a formal theological education and that it was completed in just a few months, it is truly a remarkable achievement. It is true that on a first casual reading by an unprejudiced person it may not leave a particularly good impression. And one can see how those already opposed to its point of view would find it easy to focus on the mistakes and defects. But fortunately for Fr. Antonii's point of view the majority of the Russian monks of Athos were not among the latter. To the contrary, the subsequent course of events on Mt. Athos indicates that those previously uncommitted found his book very convincing indeed.

Retaliation Against the Author of Apologiia Very

It was not convincing enough for his abbot, though. Antonii's first articles had been written and published with Abbot Jerome's blessing, and *Apologiia Very* had been begun that way, but before its completion Jerome radically changed his stand. That apparently occurred as follows. During June and July, Fr. Aleksei Kireyevsky made several trips to St. Andrew's in an unsuccessful attempt at convincing Jerome to put a stop to Fr. Antonii's "propaganda." Then on July 19 he brought a letter from Abp. Antonii in which the latter expressed great anger not only at Fr. Antonii Bulatovich but also at Jerome himself for printing Fr. Antonii's works in the skete's journal. Others then warned the abbot that the powerful archbishop would probably one day be metropolitan or even patriarch and would in retaliation expropriate St. Andrew's dependencies in St. Petersburg and Odessa. It seems likely that such arguments along with the archbishop's own words did have an influence upon Jerome; in any case, soon thereafter he prohibited Fr. Antonii from continuing to write and from associating with the monks from New Thebaide. Fr. Antonii refused to obey and so on July

26/August 8, 1912 was obliged to leave St. Andrew's. He was taken in by the nearby cell of the Annunciation located less than a mile from St. Andrew's, from which he continued his work unhindered.

Fr. Jerome began active opposition to the imiaslavtsy. He called in for personal discussions those he suspected of sharing Fr. Ilarion's and Fr. Antonii's views and even confiscated copies of *Na Gorakh Kavkaza* and burned them. It is about one of those discussions that the most famous single anecdote of the whole controversy is told: he is said to have emphasized his point in an argument by writing the name "Jesus" on a piece of paper, throwing it on the ground, and stomping on it, saying "There's your God!" Jerome himself later denied having done that, but his opponents claimed to have eyewitnesses. For his part, Fr. Antonii was not inclined to mince words and entitled one pamphlet written around that time "The New Demon-talk (*besoslovie*) of the Imiabortsy." That work Fr. Jerome eventually countered with an "open letter" disavowing any agreement with the teachings set forth in it and in all Fr. Antonii's other writings (text in Kliment, 759-60). But he did not specify what those teachings were, and such a short disavowal relying on pastoral authority and completely devoid of theological proofs finally proved no match for Fr. Antonii's "propaganda" devoid of the former and full of the latter.

3
Imiaslavtsy Victorious

The Ecumenical Patriarch Enters the Fray

During the summer of 1912 the leadership of the Rossikon (another name for St. Panteleimon's monastery) also took a firm stand against the imiaslavtsy. On August 20/September 2 Abbot Misail, among whose closest advisors was Agafodor, thought to bring the quarreling to an end by having the entire brotherhood sign one "confession of faith" that would presumably settle the matter once and for all. After beginning with the standard Nicene creed this document added:

> When we pronounce his all-holy and divine name, i.e. Jesus Christ, we represent to ourselves the invisible presence of himself, our Lord God and Savior Jesus Christ, the second person of the Holy Trinity, neither separating his name, nor confusing. In which [i.e. in the name of Jesus] we must be saved, but we must honor him [i.e. only Jesus himself] and worship the Lord God himself (qtd. in Komnenos 365-6).

This was obviously created by a person who shared Khrisanf's point of view; the statement that "we must be saved in the name" (from Acts 4:12) was a sop to the imiaslavtsy, while the main thrust was the implication that the name is not to be honored or worshiped.

This confession was presented to each monk of the monastery to sign individually in the presence of the council of twelve elders with the abbot. Under such conditions most dared not do otherwise, but a certain Fr. Dositheus insisted on being given a copy of it to take and examine at his leisure, which request was reluctantly granted. He then carried it off to Fr. Antonii Bulatovich at the cell of the Annunciation, where his suspicions of its unacceptability were confirmed.

Perhaps because of this latest impasse, both sides in the dispute finally decided to appeal to the ecclesiastical authority common to them all – the patriarch of Constantinople (Istanbul). Fr. Antonii sent to Patr. Joachim III a letter (see Komnenos 363-4). Misail sent the monk Kirik, apparently an activist on the side of Aleksei and Agafodor, along with a copy of *Na Gorakh Kavkaza*. Since he knew no Russian, the patriarch's ability to investigate the issues was limited, and since he could naturally be expected to pay more attention to the personal arguments of the representative of a great monastery than to one short letter of a simple and unknown monk, his response was predictable.

In a letter dated September 2, 1912 (see *Hoi Iēsouanoi*) and addressed to Abbot Misail and all Athonite monks "Russian by race," the patriarch warned all those who had invented a "false theory" about "the divinity of the name 'Jesus'" to cease from their "ignorant theologizing" and "soul-destroying error" and instead to attend to the salvation of their own souls. The solution to whatever misunderstandings they have is to be found in the traditional teaching of the Church, "beyond or besides which no one has the right to innovate and say something new." Since the cause of the "scandal" is the book of Ilarion, which contains many "expressions about the name 'Jesus'" which are "false, leading to error and heresy," its reading is forbidden to all who live on the Holy Mountain. More severe measures are promised to follow in the case of persistence and disobedience on the part of those disseminating the "ignorant and blasphemous teaching."

Misail arranged to have the letter translated into Russian, read publicly at a special meeting of the brotherhood of the Rossikon, copied, and disseminated throughout Russian Athos. The Russian translation, while usually faithful to the Greek, contained one noteworthy misrepresentation which betrayed the attitude of its translators. Where the patriarch had warned that no one is permitted to "innovate and say something new" (*neoterizein kai kainofonein*), the Russian text read "innovate and use new expressions" (*novshestvovat' i novye vyrazheniia upotrebliat'*). The difference between these phrases is substantial. One can use the same old expressions to say something essentially new – as when monophysites used St. Cyril's "one nature in Christ" to deny Jesus Christ's humanity. And one can use new expressions to say something that had been implicit – as when the term "Trinity" or the phrase "two natures in Christ" came into use. This mistranslation simplified matters for those siding with Khrisanf, for they could easily show that Ilarion's "expression" was new, whereas to prove that it **meant** something essentially new and therefore foreign to the faith was another matter.

Although the Patriarch's letter was presented as a condemnation of the imiaslavtsy, it did not serve that purpose well. To begin with, it was extremely vague and ambiguous. While condemning certain "expressions," Joachim never said which ones they were, nor did he in any way specify the content of the "false theory." Fr. Antonii could and did interpret them as referring rather to such expressions as Khrisanf's "mediating power" or to his attributing the name "Jesus" only to the Lord's human nature. This is hardly what the patriarch intended, but then by leaving the issues unspecified he had left his letter open to such interpretations. Probably he had hoped mainly to foster peace among the Russian monks of Athos without having to invest the time and effort necessary for a detailed investigation of complicated theological issues. Not having performed that investigation, he was careful to avoid saying anything that could later turn out to be wrong. Hence the ambiguous wording. Hence also his failure to resolve the problem and secure the hoped-for peace. The genuine theological issues that were the true cause of the unrest remained unaddressed, and a mere order to "stop talking about it" would not make them go away.

Moreover, although it was heralded as an official dogmatic decree in which the very authority of the church itself had spoken, Fr. Antonii could convincingly argue that in truth it was more like a private letter: it didn't have the signature of the patriarch and the bishops in his synod; it didn't have the patriarch's official seal; it didn't have the headings and initial greetings customary for such official decrees; and it had been addressed directly to Misail instead of to the *Iera Koinotes* ("Sacred Community"; also called the Protat), the central governing assembly of the Holy Mountain.

Trouble Brews at St. Andrew's Skete

A relative calm followed the reception of this letter, but it appears to have been due as much to Fr. Aleksei's departure for Jerusalem as to the letter itself. (A visiting Russian hierarch, vicar-bishop of Moscow Trifon, reportedly advised Fr. Misail to send him away for that purpose.) The calm did not last. On December 2 more than one hundred monks in a "council" held at New Thebaide unanimously proclaimed their belief that God's name truly is God himself, and they condemned Khrisanf's review as heretical and blasphemous. That decision was reached peacefully, but in another month the imiaslavtsy won a similar victory at St. Andrew's in a complex series of events involving fist-fights and excommunications.

In November of 1912 Abbot Jerome left St. Andrew's to attend to affairs at the skete's dependency "Nuzla" in Macedonia, apparently convinced that he had adequately dealt with those inclined toward Ilarion's views. In fact, he had succeeded rather in stirring up active opposition to himself as well as to his theological position, and his opponents used his unusually long absence of seven weeks to their advantage. A few took the lead in this work, talking to uncommitted monks, passing around copies of Fr. Antonii's writings, and even arranging to have scriptural and patristic texts glorifying the name of God be read at meal times.[14] They spread around copies of Jerome's open letter to Fr. Antonii, arguing that since he had personally approved the publication of Fr. Antonii's first article, but in the letter denied any agreement with the views presented in all his writings, one could only conclude that it was he who had changed his views. Formerly Orthodox, he was no longer so. During December the squabbling degenerated to the degree that someone wrote and passed around a note warning that "During dinner they will bang on the plates, and directly after this all those on Jerome's side will begin to be beat up." However, both sides claimed the other wrote the note, and at the sparsely attended dinner that day no beatings occurred.

At any rate, by the time Jerome returned on January 8/21 the tide had turned against him, and he found a large number of monks unwilling even to approach him for the customary

---

[14] During meals at monasteries all are silent while one person reads a text chosen for its spiritually edifying value.

blessing. Jerome called the three monks he determined to be ringleaders in marshalling sentiment against him to an assembly of the twelve *epitropoi* (the governing body charged with aiding an abbot in his administration of a skete or monastery). The intention was to take disciplinary measures, but when he called upon the members of the council to condemn and expel the "rebels" from the skete, the latter exclaimed that they did not recognize the council's authority because its most senior member was not present. That was the ancient Archimandrite David, a man highly honored among the brotherhood for his status as one of the skete's founders (he had contributed millions of rubles to building it up) and for his long forty-five year presence there. Whether his not being invited had been because his sympathies for the imiaslavtsy were known or because, as a partisan of Jerome later claimed, he was not actually an epitropos at the time is difficult to determine now. The former seems likely, for Jerome acceded to their demand and summoned Fr. David.

This time when Jerome again read the charges against the three, a young monk who was present neither as one of the judges nor as one of those being tried (presumably his job was to serve coffee or take notes) suddenly spoke up, excitedly accusing Jerome himself of blasphemy and heresy. After that,

> ... a heavy silence reigned for several minutes. Finally, having recovered from the interruption, Fr. Jerome sensed that it had become necessary not to condemn [others] but to defend himself and said in a quiet voice to Fr. David, "I hear that you call me a heretic."
>
> "I not only call [you that], but here at the council I affirm that you are a heretic, a blasphemer of the name of God," replied David. An altercation began, which ended with Fr. David leaving the conference hall and exclaiming, "Flee, brothers; our abbot is a

heretic.[15] Before the whole council he repudiated Jesus." (*Moia bor'ba*, 134-5)

This striking remark was directed to the large crowd of monks that had gathered outside the hall waiting to see the outcome, and coming as it did from such an authoritative figure it made quite an impression. Actually Jerome had taken pains to deny having made just such a repudiation, responding directly to claims that he had changed his originally Orthodox opinions:

> [He] answered to this that in that letter [to Fr. Antonii] he had written that he does not acknowledge the teaching of Bulatovich – but not that he repudiates the Lord Jesus Christ, in whom he believes and confesses that he – our Lord Jesus Christ – is the true God [and] that his name is holy, awesome, [and] worthy of worship. But although he has such a reverent attitude toward it – toward the name of God – he does not divinize it.
>
> "But I confess that the name Jesus is God himself with [his] essence and with all his characteristics," said Fr. David.
>
> "And when the name 'Jesus son of Nave or son of Sirach' occurs in divine scripture, then what do you think?" asked Abbot Jerome.
>
> "Of course, then it isn't God."
>
> "Then why are you arguing?" (Kliment, 764)

In part what was at work here was the unwillingness of either side to try to understand the other. The imiaslavtsy could reasonably argue that a denial of the divinity of the Lord's name implied or would inevitably lead to a denial of his own divinity,

---

[15] Others report that he said, "... our abbot is a Mason ..."; however, for the monks the difference in meaning would not be terribly significant.

but those doing so did not consciously make that connection. So a statement like Fr. David's was something of an oversimplification and misrepresentation even if, as Fr. Antonii suggests, all were aware of the particulars of the controversy and would have understood that in saying "he repudiated Jesus" David meant "he repudiated Jesus' name."

The next morning, in order to defend his own reputation Jerome called a meeting of the senior monks of the skete, about sixty in all. He explained that the accusations against him were groundless slander; affirmed that he had never changed his beliefs; read the creed to prove his Orthodoxy; and even repeated his expressions of respect for God's name. But a certain Fr. Sergius loudly accused him of having "repudiated Jesus" on the previous day. Then during the ensuing altercation a large crowd of uninvited junior monks began to enter through the unlocked doors, and as they filled the hall the meeting quickly turned into a series of vehement accusations of heresy and blasphemy directed against Jerome. Finally the senior epitropos asked the brotherhood, "Well, what do you want?" and received the reply "We want a change of abbot." Jerome reportedly then remarked "Well, do with me as you will," and left the hall.

Ethnic Rivalries on Mt. Athos

Since the skete's charter stipulated that if the brotherhood became dissatisfied with their abbot they could remove him and elect another by a simple majority vote, many felt the first stage had already been achieved. So the leaders of the party of imiaslavtsy felt empowered to immediately call back Fr. Antonii Bulatovich, who upon leaving back in July of 1912 had given a written promise not to return except at the request of abbot and brotherhood. He came immediately and assumed the lead in all of the following events. The next day, January 10/23, a meeting of the whole brotherhood was called to confirm its deposition of Fr. Jerome. Unanimous assent to this was confirmed by acclamation (it seems that those on Jerome's side simply did not attend), and two tables were presented with petitions to which those present were invited to affix their signatures. One read:

> I the undersigned believe and confess that the name of God and the name of the Lord Jesus Christ is holy by itself (*samo po sebe*), is inseparable from God, and is God himself, as is confessed by many holy fathers. Blasphemers and despisers of the Lord's name I reject as heretics, and therefore I request the removal of the abbot Jerome. (*Moia bor'ba*, 141)

The other read:

> We the undersigned, having lost love and trust for our abbot, Archimandrite Jerome, request his removal.

According to Fr. Antonii two different forms were used due to distrust of the Greeks.

The cause for that distrust may be found in the political history of Mt. Athos. Although always under the direct spiritual authority of the Ecumenical Patriarch, the Holy Mountain had long been governed locally by a body of representatives quartered in the town of Karyes. The method of choosing these representatives varied until the seventeenth century when the present system was instituted, according to which each of twenty "ruling monasteries" sends one representative to that council (called the *Iera Koinotes*). Every other monastic institution on the Mountain, from tiny hermitages to large communities of hundreds of monks, then came under the direct authority of one of these twenty monasteries. The "twenty" became so entrenched in their positions that other monasteries established later could not even be called by that name but rather had to be called "sketes" in recognition of their subordinate relationship to whatever ruling monastery they happened to be under. As might be expected, over time some "monasteries" declined almost to extinction while some "sketes" grew larger than most of the "monasteries" – yet the decrepit monastery always maintained full political power over the bustling skete due to the antiquated political system.

Being located in Greece, Athos has long been inhabited primarily by Greeks, but as it eventually became a monastic center for all of the Orthodox world, other ethnic groups established their own monasteries there – Bulgarians, Rumanians, Georgians, and Serbians, as well as Russians. The latter were among the last to come to Athos in significant numbers so at first had no political power on the peninsula. But soon they outnumbered the Greeks at one of the twenty ruling monasteries, installed a Russian abbot, and turned it into an officially and exclusively Russian monastery. That was the Rossikon, and it grew to be the largest on Athos, with a population at its peak of around 1,700 monks. The Russians continued to immigrate, and they built two other large monasteries which, being new, had to be placed under the direct authority of (Greek) ruling monasteries and so had to be called "sketes." These were the sketes of St. Elijah and St. Andrew. Each was comprised of several hundred monks, a number greater than that of many of the ruling monasteries. During the nineteenth century Russians continued to fill many other smaller monastic settlements and hermitages, their numbers eventually exceeding even that of the Greeks. Yet with all these changes they still had only a one twentieth say in governing the affairs of the peninsula. And so the Russians resented the Greeks for maintaining political power and using it to their advantage though being numerically in the minority.

The Greeks in turn resented the Russians. They felt like a small nation about to be swallowed up by a gigantic imperialist power and resented the fact that many of their financial resources, largely in the form of wealthy pilgrims who would leave donations behind them, were being diverted from their own monasteries to those of the Russians. That was an unavoidable eventuality since the wealthiest Orthodox country was Russia, and most of the wealthy pilgrims were Russian.

Then suddenly in November of 1912 Athos was freed by Greece from the political control of the Ottoman Empire, an event both sides saw to be fraught with both danger and opportunity. The Turks had at least been neutral in Russo-Greek squabbles, but the Russians feared that such would not be the case if the Greek state took political control of Athos. Therefore the Russian government proposed to the Greek government a plan for giving control of Athos to an international protectorate under a consortium of six Orthodox countries, naturally with Russia at its head. The Russian monks of Athos supported the plan wholeheartedly and made no secret of their intention to use it as an opportunity to remedy inequities in the Holy Mountain's system of local government. Ideally they hoped to institute a direct-election system whereby each monk would have one vote, but they at least hoped to raise their two large sketes of St. Elijah and St. Andrew to the status of ruling monasteries.

Initially the Greek government was inclined to go along with the Russian plan, but upon encountering vociferous opposition to the idea from the Greek monasteries of Athos, it decided to leave the decision up to the conference of Great Powers being held in London. To that conference the Greek monasteries sent delegations lobbying against the international protectorate and in favor of making Athos part of the Greek state. The Russian monastery sent its own delegation arguing in favor of the international protectorate and against making Athos part of the Greek state. And so Russo-Greek tensions on Athos were at an all-time high during the very period of this theological controversy.

St. Andrew's was subordinated to the Greek monastery Vatopedi, so any action as important as replacing the abbot required its official approval. And the imiaslavtsy were concerned that if the Greeks became aware that behind the events at St. Andrew's was a theological controversy, they would use it against the Russians in any way they could. Besides that, it was felt that the Greeks' low level of spiritual life disqualified them from acting as judges in a theological controversy anyway. And since for the removal of an abbot the skete's charter required only the brotherhood's dissatisfaction with him, the second petition citing "loss of love and trust" was all that had to be explained to Vatopedi. The first explaining the theological reasons was to be sent later to the Russian Holy Synod for confirmation of its validity.

Both petitions were signed by 302 monks, with only 70 refusing. An impressive margin, but perhaps due in part to a degree of coercion since each monk had to approach the table in the presence of the entire brotherhood and publicly sign or not sign. Given the obviously strong feelings of a vocal majority (or even minority) it would take a strong-willed person not to do so, and one may imagine that there could have been some among the 302 who simply found signing the easiest route to take. Had a secret ballot been used as was stipulated in the charter, the results might have been more favorable for Jerome.

A similar process was used for choosing the new abbot. Fr. Antonii says he at first suggested nominating candidates and choosing among them by secret ballot, but then:

> The elders and the whole brotherhood in one voice objected, "What other candidates are there, we all ask for Fr. David." "Whoever wants Fr. David – move over to the right; whoever doesn't want him, move to the left" exclaimed Fr. Sergius, and all three hundred persons turned up on the right side. (*Moia bor'ba*, 141)

The process of getting confirmation for these proceedings from Vatopedi turned out not to be so simple.

Immediately after the meeting on the morning of the ninth at which the brotherhood had expressed its desire to remove him, Jerome had dispatched to Vatopedi a complaint charging his opponents with rebellion and heresy. Vatopedi then sent four representatives to investigate, who arrived that evening while the meeting to choose Jerome's successor was going on. They began their investigation by talking to Jerome and his partisans. In those conversations, as later in writing, Jerome resorted to a misrepresentation of his opponents' position similar in nature to the way some of them had misrepresented his own. He claimed that David "stubbornly affirms that the very name of the second hypostasis of the Holy Trinity is God himself by essence ..." (see *Moia bor'ba*, 145-6). This clearly implied a position confusing the name as letters and sounds with the essence of God, something none of the imiaslavtsy ever advocated. In any case, whether they were convinced by this or by his appeals to the condemnations of *Na Gorakh Kavkaza* made by Abp. Antonii and Patr. Joachim, Vatopedi's representatives were inclined to side with Jerome.

The imiaslavtsy were unpleasantly surprised to learn of the Greeks' presence when the latter asked to interview the leaders of the former. They consented to speak with them, but to questions about theological issues they merely responded that they had become dissatisfied with Jerome, that that was all the skete's charter required, and that that was all Vatopedi needed to know. Moreover, the skete's charter had been designed to minimize Greek interference in Russian affairs and specified that representatives from Vatopedi could come only in response to an official request signed by the abbot and four epitropoi – so they were there illegally. Recognizing the truth of that, the Greeks started treating the "rebels" more respectfully, gave up trying to discuss theology with them, and merely specified some changes in format for the petitions concerning Fr. David's election. The new petitions were duly signed on the eleventh at a meeting observed by the monks from Vatopedi and to the procedures of which they expressed no objections. But their sympathies were with Jerome, and when they left later that day they carried with them a written complaint from him signed by seventy monks of St. Andrew's.

The delegation of four from St. Andrew's, headed by Fr. Antonii himself, which was then sent to Vatopedi to seek confirmation of David as abbot was aware neither of those sentiments nor of that complaint. Some difficulties were expected since Jerome's refusal to give up the key to the skete's vault had made it impossible to validate their petitions with its official seal, but the response they actually met with was completely unexpected.

All seemed to go well at first. They were received with honor by Vatopedi's governing council of twelve and were told that all was in order despite some dissatisfaction with the absence of the skete's seal on the petitions and the fact that the election had not been by secret ballot. Then they were given a sealed envelope which they were told contained all that had been said at the meeting and included a promise to send representatives to ceremonially install David as abbot in the near future. They had not been shown the letter itself, though, and were advised not to open the envelope until they got back to St. Andrew's.

Fr. Antonii suspected foul play in such a request, so decided to open it anyway – and found his suspicions justified. In the letter, Vatopedi objected strongly to the election's having been conducted "not by the rules and customs of the skete" but "in such a way that is used nowhere in the world, for this way is considered by all to be coercive". (Kliment, 771) It advised the brotherhood to consider Jerome as orthodox and warned that Fr. Antonii and all those accepting the "new faith" taught by *Na Gorakh Kavkaza* would be condemned, excommunicated, and expelled from the Holy Mountain. On the other hand, while suggesting that the brotherhood "drive from the skete this heresy of Ieromonakh Antonii Bulatovich,"[16] it did not identify David as a heretic. And in advising them to go ahead and choose a new abbot in the correct manner by secret ballot it at least tacitly affirmed the legality of Jerome's deposition.

---

[16]Some printed versions insert a comma that changes the meaning to "... drive out this heresy, [and] Fr. Antonii Bulatovich ..."

A Melee at St. Andrew's Skete

The representatives from St. Andrew's complained to the Vatopedi authorities, but the latter were only angry that their directions had not been followed. They stood firm in their decision. So a disappointed party of four set out for home on January 12/25, recognizing that despite a partially favorable decision they had been placed in an impossible predicament. Although they had been granted the right to choose a new abbot, whomever they chose could never be confirmed. Jerome would need only accuse the new abbot and his supporters of believing the heresy taught by *Na Gorakh Kavkaza* and they would be back to square one. While discussing this hopeless situation on the way back, the group was met by a messenger with news that Jerome's partisans were going from cell to cell talking to relatively uncommitted monks, and he was gaining more supporters hourly.[17] Fr. Antonii recounts his thoughts at that moment:

> An agonizing question – "What to do?" – oppressed the soul. If the party of Jerome gained the upper hand, imiaborchestvo would triumph completely over the whole holy mountain too. The most zealous confessors of the orthodox confession of faith in the divine dignity of the name of the Lord would be driven away, the more faint-hearted would be oppressed and forced into a repudiation ... But where to seek a defense? Where to seek a just judge? (*Moia bor'ba*, 150)

Fr. Antonii prayed for guidance and asked his companions for advice. Fr. Sergius' suggestion that they simply drive out Jerome

---

[17] Supposedly through bribery and/or threats, but both sides were remarkably free with such accusations. There may have been a grain of truth in them but if so it is likely a small one.

was rejected at first, but then as they reached the skete and heard more about Jerome's increasing strength, he thought again:

> It was necessary to act. The brotherhood had entrusted themselves to me and expected a decision from me. It was impossible to delay, for with each second of delay the situation could only get worse and more complicated and bring the sides to the point where each would arm itself with what it could, and the matter would go as far as the shedding of blood. In this moment as I thought, a deacon suggested, "Well, what then, Father, purge?" "Vox populi – vox Dei." I thought to myself, and decisively answered, "Yes, yes, purge." (151)

With that he and about thirty or forty of his most zealous followers rushed to the abbot's cell. Jerome was ready for him. When Vatopedi had given Fr. Antonii the aforementioned letter, they had also sent one of their own couriers on ahead to St. Andrew's to give Jerome a copy. The courier had found imiaslavtsy guarding the gate[18] and was not allowed access, but some of Jerome's partisans had yelled to him from a balcony to ask what he had come for. Upon learning who they were he had read aloud to them the contents of the letter. And so Fr. Antonii and his followers found Fr. Jerome in his meeting hall sitting behind his desk and surrounded by a crowd of his own followers confident of their own position in the dispute.

Upon entering, Fr. Antonii turned to an icon of the Theotokos, crossed himself and prayed a short prayer, then turned to Fr. Jerome and asked if he would voluntarily

---

[18] Athonite monasteries are built like medieval castles, i.e., like one massive building with a large courtyard in the center where the church and often other buildings are located. There is usually one main gate which serves as the only way in.

acknowledge his deposition and leave the abbot's cell. Jerome responded that he, Antonii, himself did not belong in, and had no part in, St. Andrew's skete, having voluntarily left it back in July. To Jerome's "you left ... you're not ours ..." the imiaslavtsy cried out "Ours! Ours! Fr. Antonii is ours!" Fr. Antonii repeated his question. Jerome asked, "Where is the paper? Show me the paper." This, of course, Fr. Antonii was not inclined to do. He asked a third time if Jerome would voluntarily give up his office. The answer was negative.

Fr. Antonii turned once more for a brief prayer toward an icon of the Mother of God, then after a period of silence crossed himself and said "In the name of the Father and of the Son and of the Holy Spirit ... **URA!**" and leaped towards the abbot's desk. Two of Jerome's men, Gabriel and Jacob by name, immediately seized him and began to choke him, and at that some from Fr. Antonii's side responded by attacking those two. An eyewitness reports:

> They gave Gabriel a whack and he in a rage let go of Fr. Antonii. Then Fr. Athanasius threw himself on Jacob and, grabbing him by the beard, dragged him away from Fr. Antonii, and the latter remained unhurt. At this point the brothers were filled with excessive anger and rushed "To URA!" There was a great fight from both sides. At first with fists, and then they started dragging each other by the hair. (Kosvintsev, 151)

Fr. Antonii once again with a cry of "URA!" rushed at the abbot's desk. Again he was attacked and again his attackers were dragged out of the room. He recounts that this was repeated several times:

> ... two of the stronger imiaslavtsy applied the following method: they ran to throw themselves upon one of the Jeromeites standing

against me and grabbed him either by the sleeve or by the hair. After dragging him out into the corridor and handing him on to others, they would run back to drag out another . (*Moia bor'ba*, 153)

What happened to those dragged out is described by the same eyewitness quoted before:

> They began to drag out of this heap [of fighting monks] one person at a time into the corridor, where the brotherhood stood in two lines, receiving the booty and passing it (Jeromeites) on: one by the hair another by the side and with a command, another they would beat for something to teach him a lesson. In this way they brought them to the stairs and then they let them down the stairs variously as each pleased: some went head first and some went feet first, counting the steps with the back of their head. They led them to the church square, then ceremoniously took them by the hand and led them out the gate. (Kosvintsev, 151)

Many of the "Jeromeites" were beaten as well as expelled, in recompense not only for their blasphemy against God's name but also for other grievances against them, as the monks expressed physically a variety of pent-up frustrations with their leadership.[19] Meanwhile Jerome himself, seeing the ranks of his supporters getting thin and recognizing the hopelessness of his position, finally consented to leave voluntarily. He was not treated roughly. Though offered a cell of his own within the

---

[19]There do not seem to have been any injuries worse than bruises and loss of hair, though there is an unconfirmed report of someone suffering a broken leg. As for Fr. Antonii's role in the fight, he did not know about the beatings and expulsions taking place behind him and put a stop to them when he found out. His feigned attack and cry of "URA" he explains was merely designed to give those behind him the courage to do the required task; he himself never laid a hand on anyone.

skete he chose to leave, joining fifteen others who had been forcibly expelled and two others who were leaving voluntarily as he was. Fr. Antonii saw him off:

> When he had gone out of the gates, Fr. Jerome turned, crossed himself, and then, prostrating himself to the ground toward me, said, "Forgive." Together with him stood Fr. Clement, who did the same and said, "Forgive." I too did to them a prostration to the ground and asked forgiveness, and they left for Karyes. (*Moia bor'ba*, 154)

The first eighteen were followed in the course of the following months by about thirty more who left or were expelled. All were taken in by other Slavic monastic communities around Athos.

St. Andrew's and St. Panteleimon's in the Hands of the Imiaslavtsy

On January 14/27 a new meeting of the whole brotherhood was called to fulfill Vatopedi's request for an election by secret ballot, but once again Fr. David was chosen by acclamation. That evening two representatives set out for Vatopedi with 307 signatures amassed in David's favor. This time they were given a letter stating that although Vatopedi remained dissatisfied with the open balloting, it nevertheless recognized the election's canonicity and promised to send representatives on the nineteenth to officially install Fr. David.

Meanwhile a similar chain of events was taking place at the Rossikon and culminated in a general meeting of the brotherhood on January 23/February 5. At that meeting, called and controlled by the imiaslavtsy who were led by a certain Fr. Ireney, the entire brotherhood of the monastery signed a confession of faith nearly identical to the one signed at St. Andrew's. Even Abbot Misail signed, presumably not wanting to share the fate of Jerome. At the same meeting the imiaslavtsy pronounced disciplinary measures against eight of their most active opponents, consisting in expulsion from the monastery for terms from one year to permanent. Kosvintsev describes the reactions to this turn of events:

> The monastery celebrated this day like Holy Pascha. The brotherhood greeted one another with kisses and exclamations of "Christ is Risen!" They cried from joy. The whole day the bell never stopped its festive ringing. This day was justly called "the triumph of orthodoxy." (471)

The rejoicing was to be short-lived. Although the imiaslavtsy had gained commanding majorities among the simple Russian monks, the higher ecclesiastical and civil authorities – both Russian and Greek – were against them. Counter-measures had begun even before the celebration at St. Panteleimon's on January 23.

4
Imiaslavtsy Under Siege

Retaliation Against St. Andrew's

Immediately on the twelfth of January Jerome mailed to the Russian embassy in Constantinople a written report of the "rebellion." A copy of it he sent to the embassy in Thessalonica along with one of his most zealous supporters, the monk Clement, who returned ten days later with Vice-consul Shcherbina. The latter, having heard and believed only one side of the story, went to St. Andrew's not to investigate but to demand that the brotherhood take back Jerome as abbot as well as all of the expelled monks. They adamantly refused. They would concede to giving Jerome a kind of severance pay of five thousand rubles, would give one hundred rubles to each of the others, and would consider accepting back some of them in a year's time if they would repent – but there could be no question of accepting Jerome back as abbot.

Threatened "punishments" were then carried out. The Russian foreign ministry instituted a "blockade" of St. Andrew's intended to force it to capitulate, a move generally attributed to the decision and authority of Russian Ambassador to Constantinople Girs and effected locally through Shcherbina. All mail going to or coming from St. Andrew's was cut off. Money being sent to the skete, even to individual members of it, was redirected to Jerome instead. The Greek port authorities were ordered not to allow St. Andrew's provisions already received and in storage to be delivered to the skete or even to be given to any of its members who would come to pick them up. When two monks were later sent to Constantinople to purchase food for St.

Andrew's, they were arrested and their twenty thousand rubles confiscated. At first the consequences for the skete were not great, but in the ensuing months its food and financial resources began to run out, and it found itself in a serious predicament. It was not until May, more than three months later, that Fr. Antonii's intervention with the Russian Ministry of External Affairs in St. Petersburg resulted in Girs's orders being countermanded.

As has been seen, Jerome's complaints had also been received sympathetically by Vatopedi. Its representatives who had arrived at St. Andrew's on the ninth had pretended to accept as in good order the deposition and replacement of Jerome but actually were on his side, arguing in his behalf after returning and bringing back with them his written complaint. Not only that, but while still at St. Andrew's they had sent a letter to the Protat (the council at Karyes) informing it that "those around the heresiarch Ieroskhimonakh Antonii forced the fathers of the skete to swear to a new dogma concerning the divinity of Jesus ..." (Papoulidis, *Hoi Rōsoi*, 79) The Vatopedi authorities' double-dealing on the twelfth of January has already been recounted, and they acted similarly on the fourteenth. On the same day when they gave the representatives from St. Andrew's a letter promising to come in a few days to install David as abbot, they sent another to the Protat, in which they listed the names of twenty-six "rebel monks" and requested that police be sent to arrest them and send them off to Thessalonica for judgment. When on the eighteenth an embassy from St. Andrew's was sent to Vatopedi to conduct its officials back to their skete for the installation of Fr. David, they were informed that due to a request from the Russian embassy in Thessalonica, Vatopedi would delay it for several days. The officials never came and David's election as abbot was never officially approved.

Having received these letters from Vatopedi as well as letters and personal pleas from Jerome after the events of the twelfth, the *Iera Koinotes* itself joined the fray. It had sent police to St. Andrew's immediately on the day of the expulsions, but by the time they arrived the fighting was over, the gate was locked, and they were not admitted to the skete. In the succeeding days a four-member delegation composed of monks from four different monasteries was sent there twice to investigate but each time was locked out. A permanent police guard was set on the besieged skete. Meanwhile the Protat was still hearing from Jerome, from Vatopedi, and from other expelled monks charges of heresy against Fr. David, Fr. Antonii, and their followers. It sent a letter to St. Andrew's asking that the skete's monks come to Karyes for an investigation into these charges (since the Protat's investigators had not been permitted to enter the skete). It received in response a letter from St. Andrew's requesting that the *Iera Koinotes* identify the accuser and the charges in writing, to which the skete would in turn respond in writing.

To that the Protat finally responded with an official letter on January 29/February 11 excommunicating the entire brotherhood of St. Andrew's. The letter did not specify the doctrinal reasons for the decision but mentioned only that it was "a religious quarrel concerning the second person of the Holy Trinity"; that the confession signed on the tenth and sent to the Russian Holy Synod was evidence of their unorthodoxy (*kakodoxia*); that Jerome seemed quite orthodox to them though called a heretic by the rebels; and that the rebels were guilty of upsetting the order and calm of the Holy Mountain. Therefore from then until an ecclesiastical court could be established to investigate the matter, it proclaimed Fr. David, Fr. Antonii, and the entire brotherhood of St. Andrew's to be unorthodox. And in order to prevent the evil's spread it warned that henceforth anyone having any contact with them would also be considered unorthodox. The announcement was to be proclaimed by posting it on the skete's main gate.

St. Andrew's replied with a letter explaining that the issue was not "a doctrine about the second person of the Holy Trinity" but the dishonoring of God's name; the skete had not received the Iera Koinotes's representatives for fear Jerome would come and cause trouble; and it would be glad to send its representatives to Karyes if it were first given a written safe-conduct (this out of fear that Antonii and David would be arrested). In conclusion it affirmed that it did indeed desire reconciliation with the I.K. But the latter was not in a conciliatory mood; it not only refused the request for a written safe-conduct, but also added that no reconciliation would be possible until the brotherhood of St. Andrew's would repudiate its unorthodoxy in writing. Predictably, no rapprochement was ever effected between the imiaslavtsy of St. Andrew's and the *Iera Koinotes*.

Jerome and the I.K. were in contact with Constantinople as well, where a new patriarch, Germanos V, had replaced Joachim III. In an official letter to the I.K. dated February 15, the patriarch blamed Fr. David and Fr. Antonii for the proceedings at St. Andrew's, called them to Constantinople for a church court, and declared that only the former leadership of the skete was the lawful one. Fr. Antonii had already left to defend his cause in Russia and so never complied. When Fr. David finally did go to Constantinople after a couple months' delay, the old, uneducated, and relatively weak-willed monk bowed to patriarchal pressure to abjure his error and promised not to promote it any more or to act as abbot. The latter promise he kept, but a month or so after returning he went back on the former.

The I.K. also carried on a correspondence with St. Panteleimon's, similar in content to the communications with St. Andrew's. There could be no charges of "rebellion" against the latter since Misail was still abbot, but some of the eight expelled monks brought news to Karyes of heresy and anarchy at the Rossikon. And Misail himself sent a letter on the third of February stating that he had been forced to sign the January 23 confession of faith and asking for police measures against a number of monks whom he named. His own authority was so limited that he had not even been able to place the monastery's seal on his letter. Police were sent, but finding peace and all apparently in order they took no action. The I.K. was eventually able to secure an agreement from St. Panteleimon's to receive back the exiled monks, but Misail's hold on power remained tenuous at best.

Archbishop Antonii Gets Involved Again

Meanwhile Abp. Antonii had been informed of the events on Athos, and the opponents of the imiaslavtsy were encouraged by a series of personal letters sent by him that attained wide distribution and were later published. In a letter dated February 11 and addressed to one of those exiled from St. Panteleimon's named Fr. Denasy, he lamented "the strengthening of heresy, more precisely gangs of lunatics (*shaiki sumasshedshikh*) led by an ambitious hussar" (Kosvintsev, 478). Promising that a trustworthy person from the Ministry of External affairs would be sent, he added "but here the matter is not for trust but rather to bring along three companies of soldiers and lock up the scoundrels (*zakovat' nakhalov*)" and concluded:

> Of course the Bulatovichites will all be expelled and deprived of monastic rank; their victory is for two weeks. But it is sad that as a consequence of the khlystic rebellion there might occur an attempt

of the Greeks to expel from Athos all Russians, which will not be so difficult under the Greek government.

This fear that the Greeks would use the dispute as an excuse to expel all Russians from Athos was to be repeatedly expressed by others too, but there is no evidence that the Greeks of Athos ever contemplated such a thought. No doubt they would have rejoiced at a decrease in Russian numbers and influence, and some might have seen it as golden opportunity to aid that decrease, but that they either could or would use such an excuse to expel all Russians is inconceivable.

The talk of settling the matter by force was no idle threat, however. There are reports that Girs soon after the events of January 12 had unsuccessfully requested the patriarch's permission to send soldiers to Athos. Apparently permission was indeed granted later, for on April 1 the I.K. received word that the Russian embassy planned to send a high official with soldiers in the company of a patriarchal exarch in order to get rid of the troublemakers. But this time Karyes proved the impediment, asking that the expedition be delayed while it tried to settle the matter itself. The patriarch's change of heart may have come about in part due to pressure from the Russian Holy Synod; in a letter to Jerome dated March 7 Abp. Antonii assured him that the Holy Synod was not only asking Patr. Germanos to confirm his predecessor's decision in this matter, but also that he would permit it to "send to Athos a Russian archbishop for admonition of those troubled by the stupid heresy" (Pakhomy, 63).

The Ecumenical Patriarch Takes a Stand

Before giving that permission, however, Patr. Germanos had decided a more detailed investigation was in order. This he entrusted to a committee of seven professors of the patriarchal theological school in Khalke, and their answer, in the form of an official report signed by all of them, was forthcoming on March 30, 1913.[20] The report states that the committee, while lacking time to go through all the materials sent to it[21] because of their great volume and their being in Russian only, "thinks that it understood the spirit" of them, if not all the details. Speaking specifically of *Na Gorakh Kavkaza*, that spirit is mysticism, "which, as is known, emerges from a vital religious feeling and manifests living faith and love" but which all too often strays from the church's dogmas and teachings because "in the investigation and understanding of religious truths it follows the dictates of the heart and of direct feeling rather than the mind."

As for their brief exposition of what the imiaslavtsy actually believe, it is somewhat simplistic but not entirely inaccurate. It recognizes that they are not concerned solely with the name "Jesus," much less that name abstracted from his person, and that they do not speak merely of "letters and syllables." The central issue it sees to be the claims that God's names as divine revelation are energies of God and are therefore God himself:

> It is superfluous to note that such a conclusion [i.e. that God's name is God himself] agrees with the idea they formulated concerning the divine names as energies of God, but this very

---

[20]References under Gnomodotēsis. The report was signed by: Germanos P. Strenopoulos (the dean), Archimandrite Ioannes Eustratios, Archimandrite Georgiades, Deacon Basileios Stephanides, Basileios Antoniades, and Pantoleon Komnenos. Apparently only Mr. Komnenos knew Russian.

[21]Two letters from the patriarch requesting information are mentioned, one of February 15 and one of March 20; if the latter was the one asking for a formal report then they had but ten days in which to prepare it. In an introductory letter the dean of the school states that the committee met eight times.

opinion, that the names themselves are energies of God, is newly-appeared and new-sounding, and their argument that every word of God as an energy of his is not only a giver of life and spirit but is itself spirit and itself life and thus itself God – this argument applied generally leads to conclusions (i.e. "the name of Jesus is God ... every divine word in the Gospel is God himself"[22]) which, in spite of all their denials, smell of pantheism.

These are the most condemnatory words offered by the Khalke professors, and they are reminiscent of Patr. Joachim's letter in their lack of decisiveness. "New" and "smelling of pantheism" are far from "heretical" or even "false."

What's more, the report observes that the blame for the quarreling lies in part on the opposing party because it:

> ... proceeded to such an interpretation of the scriptural phrase "in which we must be saved" (Acts 4:12), as if they too believed that one is saved in the name of Jesus, as a name, but that one must not venerate (*proskynein*) the name but only Jesus himself. Thus they gave cause for opposing argument.

In conclusion it merely expresses hope that those who have chosen "the tranquil and quiet life" will stop debating and arguing and attend to sanctifying themselves in the traditional worship of the Lord Jesus Christ.

Strangely, when five days later Patr. Germanos sent his decision on the matter to Karyes in the form of an official decree, all ambivalence had been abandoned. The "newly-appeared and

---

[22]Quoting Fr. Antonii Bulatovich's August 27, 1912 letter to Patr. Joachim III. Calling words "spirit and life" was in fact not an invention of Fr. Antonii's but came directly from scripture where it is placed on the lips of Jesus: "... the words I have spoken to you are spirit and are life." (John 6:63)

vain-sounding[23] teaching" is condemned outright as "impious and soul-corrupting" and as constituting "blasphemous unorthodoxy (*kakodoxia*) and heresy". Germanos instructs the I.K. to "require on behalf of us and of the Church that all abjure completely the blasphemous error and refrain henceforth with prayer from various and foreign teachings." As for those who might refuse:

> ... concerning such [people]: being heretics and rebels against church discipline, the measures determined by the holy canons will be taken, and in no way will it be acceptable that such [people] remain and through their plague corrupt your pious place ... (See *Hoi Iēsouanoi*)

One can only conjecture at why the patriarch would so definitively condemn the imiaslavtsy just five days after receiving an ambivalent and ambiguous response from Khalke even containing a reproach for the opposing side. Some have suggested that anti-Russian sentiment was involved, and it may well be that an opportunity to lessen the Russian population of Athos seemed attractive – but to take advantage of that opportunity the patriarch almost certainly was encouraged by Russians themselves. As has been seen, there is evidence that at Abp. Antonii's prompting the Russian Holy Synod had already asked Germanos to confirm Joachim's decision. And it is known how firmly the Russian embassy in Constantinople was in favor of Jerome's side in the dispute. So it is not difficult to imagine

---

[23] The patriarch's letter reads "kenofōnos" (vain sounding) where the Khalke report read "kainofōnos" (new sounding or newly heard of). One or the other is probably a mistake: the words are easily confused because they sound identical in modern Greek.

that pressure from both sources was brought to bear on the patriarch – perhaps economic, perhaps political, perhaps both.

In any case, the epistle itself indicates that doctrinal considerations served as an excuse for the condemnation and were not the cause for it. There are but two short statements that specify the substance of the heretical teaching:

> [The teaching is] about the name "Jesus," as being Jesus himself and God and inseparable and, so to speak, hypostatically identified (*syntautizomenou*) with him ... [it is] about the name "Jesus" as being Jesus himself and God, essentially contained (*emperiekhomenou*) in his name.

The Khalke report had plainly recognized that the dispute, while primarily concerned with the name of Jesus, was really about all of God's names, but the patriarch spoke as if only "the name 'Jesus'" was at issue. And placing the name in quotes as he did suggested an emphasis on the very letters and sounds which the Khalke commission recognized was definitely not at issue. Nor did Khalke make any intimation that the imiaslavtsy were equating God's name with his essence, yet the phrase "essentially contained" blithely accuses them of idiocy. Such misrepresentations may have come from Abp. Antonii, from official communications of the Russian Holy Synod inspired by him,[24] from Jerome, from other Russian opponents of the imiaslavtsy, or even from Greek Athonites – but his choosing to use the testimony of any of those over his own best theologians can best be explained by referring to ulterior motives.

---

[24]There are, however, other reports that while trying to reach a decision Patr. Germanos twice telegraphed the Holy Synod asking for an opinion and received no reply. See Ivol'gin, *Nasha diplomatiia i Afon*.

Be that as it may, this was the official dogmatic decree long desired by Jerome, Misail, and their partisans. Unlike Joachim's letter, this one was unambiguous and met all the formal requirements for such a decree, so there could be no arguing that it was merely a private peace-making letter. And the I.K. did not take it that way. At a meeting on April 29/May 12 it declared that anyone who continued to believe the heresy would have to be expelled from the Holy Mountain. But first it had to see to the task of promulgating the patriarch's decree. In the case of the besieged fortress St. Andrew's this was no mean task – so the Protat sent a copy to Vatopedi and told them to do it.

To St. Panteleimon's a delegation of two was sent. They arrived on May 2/15 and arranged to read the epistle publicly in both Greek and Russian at a meeting of the whole brotherhood on the next day. They described the result in their report to the I.K.:

> ... during the reading calm and full silence predominated, then the monk Irenei of the heresiarchs took the stand and sought to debate about the opinion of his followers. But the *Iera Koinotes* [i.e. the delegates themselves] informed him that since there existed an ecclesiastical decision all debate was superfluous and urged them to study it, and the next day to declare if they would conform to it or not. (Papoulidis, *Hoi Rōsoi*, 104)

To them it looked like the monks were going to sign the form provided, but then the "heresiarchs" advised them not to do so, arguing that the epistle was a fake and that those at the patriarchate and at the I.K. were heretics. Other reports say that they added the numeral values of the letters in "*Khalkē*" together, didn't get what they wanted, so changed it to "*Khalkei*" (a misspelling that would sound the same) and found that it totalled 666, the mark of the antichrist. The delegates expressed dismay also that:

> To top it all they took down the venerable patriarchal epistle which was framed and printed in gold letters and prepared for public reading in the front yard of the monastery – and destroyed it. (Papoulidis, *Hoi Rōsoi*, 105)

Although the I.K. delegates said that a "sufficient number" (*hikanoi*) eventually did sign the forms affirming that they "received" the patriarchal letter and "agreed in every way with its spirit" (Papoulidis, *Hoi Rōsoi*, 107), that "sufficient number" must actually have been quite small. Or perhaps many signed merely to avoid trouble with the Karyes authorities. In any case, when another task force came in June to try to convince the imiaslavtsy to recant it was estimated that even then they constituted three fourths of the monastery's population.

The I.K. delegates called police to remove the ringleaders, but upon arrival the police found calm and peace and said that they could not do anything without orders from Thessalonica. So a permanent post of two of them was established to maintain the peace, and a request for the necessary orders was sent. Such orders never arrived, however, for the Russian church and government were taking steps of their own which would soon make Greek police superfluous.

5
The Russian Church's Decision

Debate in the Russian Press

In Russia itself, whatever squabbles over the name of God which arose apparently resolved themselves peacefully and so did not make it into the newspapers. But the spectacle of Russian monks engaging in fistfights and tearing each other's hair out – this was newsworthy. Early reports in the secular press presented woefully inaccurate accounts of both events and issues. In March some said "Andrey" Bulatovich had "organized a rebellion" not only at St. Andrew's but at St. Elijah's and St. Panteleimon's as well, expelling Abbot Misail from the latter in the process. As late as April the St. Petersburg newspaper *Rech'* carried a report that the new "heresy" counted nine persons in the Holy Trinity and that Ilarion had been Bulatovich's orderly (*denshchik*) in Ethiopia.

A few publications closely tied to church circles followed the lead of *Russkii Inok*. The one coming closest to Abp. Antonii's vehement style was the newspaper *Kolokol* (The Bell), published by an official of the Holy Synod named Vasily Mikhailovich Skvortsov (1859-1932). Skvortsov was known as the organizer of the "Internal Mission" of the Russian Orthodox Church and was often appointed by the Holy Synod to deal with sectarians, schismatics, and heretics. Seeing a new heresy in the imiaslavtsy, he had begun a series of attacks against them in *Kolokol* already in 1912. The virulence of these attacks is exemplified by a review of Fr. Antonii's *Apologiia Very* printed in 1913. Referring to the statement that even "unconscious pronunciation" of God's names is effective, the review states that:

In the foolish Apology of Bulatovich ... God doesn't have power over us but we, insignificant, sinful people, have power over him. We need only pronounce his name, even without faith, without reverence, "unconsciously," carelessly – and we will have him with all his characteristics ... What a terrible blasphemous teaching, lowering the omnipotent Master of heaven and earth to the level of an obedient tool of man ... This is magic, transferred wholly from the dark realm of the divinely renounced sciences of wizardry into the dogmatics supposedly of the orthodox faith ... (qtd. in *Sbornik dokumentov*, 47).

The book's "masked goal" is to promote "antinomianism, i.e. that there is no necessity for a moral life":

"All is sanctified by God's name" [they say], i.e. do any abominations you care to, any shameful acts you want to, but if during it you repeat the name of God all this "is sanctified"!!

Another *Kolokol* article proclaimed that:

The provenance of the new heresy, taking in view the seemingly edifying nature of the book *Na Gorakh Kavkaza* and hence its popularity – exposes the extremely cunning work of Satan, who has prepared in a completely hidden and sweet form murderous poison (qtd. In TsOV 1913 19:9).

Other papers even resorted to slander and character assassination, carrying spurious reports that among other misdeeds Fr. Antonii had married and abandoned an Ethiopian on one of his trips (see Pakhomy, 111).

Fr. Antonii, who had left Athos in February in order to defend his cause in Russia, had his work cut out for him. He began by writing letters to newspapers. Some, like *Kolokol*, would not print them, but others were sympathetic. *Moskovskiia Vedomosti* (Moscow News) on March 9 printed one of his letters on the front page and accompanied it with a long, basically sympathetic introductory article remarking that, "of course," a final decision could only take place at a church council. In a reflection of the widespread concern about the political consequences of the controversy, the paper also warned against rashly accusing Russian monks on Athos of heresy especially because that would give the Greeks the right to kick them all out, and then the Holy Mountain would be lost to Russia for good. Less than a month later the same paper devoted a large article to the story of Fr. Antonii's life – to show that he "is not at all like the picture drawn of him by his enemies, who are no less embittered in the spiritual field than on the battle fields." (Apr 5:2)

Others rendered even more substantial support. M. A. Novoselov of the Moscow "Religious-Philosophical Society" offered to take on the task of publishing *Apologiia* at his own expense, and it appeared in March. A foreword expressed strong views about the importance of the doctrinal issues at stake:

> Like the wave of an earthquake, through the whole Universal Church, from South to North, from East to West, spread indignation when some thoughtless and corrupted-by-rationalism monks dared to attack that nerve of the Church upon which converge all other nerves, that dogma, the denial of which constitutes the denial of all dogmas, that holy thing (*sviatynia*) that lies at the foundation of all holy things. (*VII*)

This was signed simply "From the Editor" (*Ot redaktsiia*), and only years later was it established as belonging to the pen of Fr. Pavel Florensky (1882-ca.1946), a well-known theologian of the Russian Church (see Andronik 288).

Fr. Florensky also asserts that *Apologiia* is but the first of many works which will be required before the church can finally decide the important issues raised. Meanwhile the controversy is itself something to be thankful for insofar as it proves that the church is not dead as many are saying – people do care about the faith after all, enough to get excited about theological issues. As for Abp. Antonii, "one can peacefully ignore" his condemnations since even the Kiev Pecherskaya Lavra saw in *Na Gorakh Kavkaza* nothing unfit to print towards the end of 1912 after months of his attacks.

Florensky quoted in its entirety a three-page letter written by "one of the most honored and accomplished theologians of our homeland" in response to the request of an also unnamed bishop for an opinion about *Apologiia*. The letter's authorship became known several years later: it was by Mitrofan Dimitriyevich Muretov (d. 1917), a professor of the Moscow Theological Academy. He echoed Florensky's positive evaluation of *Apologiia* and belief in the debate's fundamental importance:

> [The book] breathes with the spirit of true monasticism, ancient, ascetic. The matter is, of course, not as simple as the reviewer of Ilarion's book sees it. In its roots the question about the Jesus prayer and the name of the Savior extends to a primordial and not yet decided – more accurately – unfinished struggle of opposites: of idealism, or, what is the same thing, mysticism, on the one side – and nominalism, which is rationalism and materialism, on the other. ... True Christianity and the Church always stood on the ground of idealism in deciding all the questions of the faith's teachings and of life that have arisen. On the other hand, pseudo- and anti-christianity and heterodoxy always held to nominalism and rationalism. (*XI*) Idealism and realism lie at the base of the teaching about the unity of essence and the trinity of person of Divinity, about the divine-humanity of the Savior, about the sacraments, especially the eucharist, about veneration of icons, etc. And I am personally on this side. The reviewer for *Russkii Inok*

and the apologist for Fr. Ilarion are not saying one and the same thing but rather completely the opposite. (*XII*)

Those who belittle Jesus' name are guilty of a great sin:

> ... those who mock the name Jesus, whether in their soul or by their lips or on notes, etc. – all the same – they know after all just what the name expresses and to whom it relates; consequently they necessarily mock also the Savior himself. Yes, and they cannot not know [this], and no sophisms can cleanse this mocking – only repentance. For this reason blasphemy against the Spirit is not forgiven, and for every, even idle, word a person will give account. And no one, speaking in the Holy Spirit, says: Jesus is anathema (in general Jesus, without any designations – for from the moment that *Logos sarx egeneto*,[25] there is only one true Jesus – the Savior, the God-man), and no one can say Jesus is Lord except by the Holy Spirit. [1 Cor 12:3] They mocked the defenders of the name Jesus and of the Jesus prayer, of course, by thoughtlessness, or to put it more truthfully, by a lack of true Christian feeling, which can always show to true Christians the true path among all temptations and misunderstandings. This is what we also see among the simple monks. (*XIII-XIV*)

Others sharing such views were also reluctant to publicly reveal their names. In the St. Petersburg paper *Novoe Vremia* (New Time) on April 11 and May 10 appeared two articles signed by one "S. Ivol'gin" who wrote authoritatively about the Athonite disputes but whose name had never been heard before and never showed up afterwards – "apparently a pseudonym for a well-known person" (Filosofov, 300). Ivol'gin expresses hopes that the Holy Synod will not move too quickly in rendering a decision. Much debate is required first, and people should at

---

[25] "The Word became flesh."

least read *Na Gorakh Kavkaza* and *Apologiia Very* before making up their minds. If Abp. Antonii would bother to read the former even he would see that he had been deceived. (A real optimist, this Ivol'gin.) The journal *Tserkovnost'* has shown what comes of hasty condemnations – it printed some "heretical statements" of Bulatovich that later turned out to have come from St. Tikhon of Zadonsk. As for Skvortsov, his position is understandable because "a missionary needs heresies like a reporter needs events." Ivol'gin provides a long list of those who would have to be excommunicated if the imiaslavtsy are declared heretics, including even famous bishops and professors of theological academies, and warns that "It will be possible to speak not of a sect but of a *schism*":

> An unheard of event in Russia – the excommunication of bishops for heresy, but it would have to take place. One must hope in the foresight of the Synod, that it will not want to create a conflagration. Everything is revealed and is formulated by degrees. There was a time when the book of Khomiakov was considered heretical and had to be printed beyond [Russia's] borders. But now the orthodox teaching about the Church is based on it. The same thing is happening with the teaching about the divinity of the name of God. When the noise dies down its truth will become indisputable.

The Holy Synod does need to render a decision soon, says Ivol'gin, and he hopes it will merely tell the monks to stop fighting and then label their doctrine a "theologoumenon" (a theological opinion). He laments, however, that Abp. Antonii has been taking an active part in advising the Synod. Observing that the archbishop's sharp words "only sew enmity," he adds:

As for the desire that to Athos would be brought "three companies of soldiers" to "lock up the scoundrels" – this would serve as the beginning of destruction for the Russian monasteries on Athos.

Abp. Antonii responded with a letter to *Novoe Vremia*, reproduced here in full:

> In today's issue of *Novoe Vremia* words are ascribed to me which I did not speak and did not write, i.e. (*budto*), that it is necessary to put in irons the followers of Bulatovich. The articles of this author represent a series of inaccuracies. Especially interesting is the fact that the author does not say a word about what constitutes the main position or thesis of the teaching of Bulatovich. (May 12:7)

As he claimed, the archbishop had indeed not written "put in irons the followers of Bulatovich," but that wasn't even how Ivol'gin had quoted him. Ivol'gin's quote was slightly different – "lock up the scoundrels" – and that was quite accurate, as were all his other quotations from Abp. Antonii.

The charge that Ivol'gin had skirted the theological issues themselves was true, however. So Fr. Antonii Bulatovich, always eager to please his ecclesiastical superiors, was quick to provide *Novoe Vremia* those particulars. He sent it a copy of his Open Letter to Abp. Antonii of May 7, 1912 and included some pertinent comments with it:

> Abp. Antonii refused to print this letter in his journal, and, in spite of the fact that we completely clearly disproved the "divinization" by us of the name itself (letters and sounds) "Jesus," nevertheless Abp. Antonii has continued to accuse us of this until the latest time. ... Yes, the patriarch condemned us with an official decree, but he condemned us of something of which we are completely innocent, for we don't think to say that the letters and sounds of the name Jesus are "essentially" joined to divinity. ...

We are amazed at the lightness with which people condemn us, and at the reluctance with which the judges attend to investigation of the matter. ... still no one has asked, specifically what do you understand and specifically what are you saying!

Despite all this activity in the secular press, the religious journals curiously remained largely silent. Just one relatively detailed examination of the doctrinal issues was published, written by a relatively unknown priest named Kh. Grigorovich. It appeared in *Missionerskoe Obozrenie* (Missionary Observer) and offered arguments against the imiaslavtsy, as could be expected from a sister publication of *Kolokol* also belonging to Mr. Skvortsov. It raised no issues not addressed by other more important sources before or after but did distinguish itself by being one of extremely few to avoid a polemical tone.

The Russian Holy Synod Enters the Fray

The next major entry into the debate was to be that of the Holy Synod itself, where Abp. Antonii Khrapovitsky's influence bode ill for the imiaslavtsy. Ober-prokuror Vladimir K. Sabler happened to be quite close to Abp. Antonii, and this closeness was reflected in the Synod's method of reaching a decision. Purportedly to attain the "greatest possible impartiality," three persons were chosen to present independently prepared reports on the subject. One highly qualified person was available for the task, and the papers later reported that he had in fact been considered – but was rejected. That person was Bishop Theofan Bystrov of Poltava (1873-1940), who was not only widely known as the "only Russian ascetic-bishop" but also had written his doctoral dissertation on the name of God in the Old Testament. However there were also rumors that he agreed with the imiaslavtsy[26] and it seems that this disqualified him. Instead the first reporter chosen was that paragon of impartiality, Abp. Antonii himself. Second was Abp. Nikon Rozhdestvenskii (1851-1918), a man who did not even have a higher theological education.[27] His conclusions too were predictable; he was one of Sabler's partisans on the Synod, as was Abp. Antonii, and shared the conservative political views of both of them. Besides that, he had already written letters and had published at least one article against the imiaslavtsy. The third choice was a lay theologian named Sergei Troitskii (1878-1973), a seminary professor's son who had graduated from the St. Petersburg Theological Academy in 1901 and had served as a professor there ever since. Whether or not he had previously been involved in this controversy is unknown.

The reports were presented, a decision was reached, and Abp. Sergius of Finland was entrusted with the task of combining the reports into one official epistle addressed to all Russian monks. That was then approved at a special meeting on May 16/29, 1913 and was published in the May 18 issue of the Synod's journal *Tserkovnyia Vedomosti* (Church News).[28]

---

[26]Ivol'gin, for one, mentioned no names but described him in such detail that there could be no doubt as to who he meant.

[27]In Russia the basic level of education was at "seminaries," roughly equivalent to our undergraduate institutions, while the equivalent of master's degrees were granted by the theological "academies." Nikon attended seminary only.

[28]Signed by all members of the Synod: Metr. Vladimir of St. Petersburg (who chaired the May 16 meeting), Metr. Sergius of Finland (later Patr. Sergius), Abp. Antonii, Abp. Nikon, Abp. Eusebius of Vladivostok, Abp. Mikhail of Grodno, and Bp. Agapit of Yekaterinoslav. See *Bozhiei milost'iu*.

Abp. Sergius's text identifies *Na Gorakh Kavkaza* as having caused the troubles by introducing a new teaching about the name "Jesus" but stresses that the Synod does believe the Jesus prayer to be of fundamental importance in monastic life. It sees the author's goal of promoting its practice to be basically laudable. But Ilarion erred when he went beyond describing prayer and its benefits to offer his own "philosophical explanation" of how and why prayer works as it does. Specifically, his error is in seeing the name itself as saving, whereas the truth of the matter is that the essence of prayer is calling upon the Lord. It is the personal God who listens and answers as he wills; prayer is not automatically effective. The Jesus prayer is based on the principle of the blind man on the way to Jericho (Lk 18:38 and parallels), who kept on crying out to the Lord until he finally got his attention.

If the view of the imiaslavtsy were correct, the consequences for spiritual life would be unthinkable: "A person need only pronounce God's name (even without faith, even unconsciously), and God is, as it were, obligated to be with this person by his grace and to do what is characteristic of him. But this is already blasphemy!" (279) Worse, it is "magic" and "superstition." Even miracles could then be worked completely without faith. And monks would be encouraged to engage in simple mechanical repetition of prayers for the mere sake of repetition, forgetting that there is a person to whom they are speaking.

The epistle refutes contentions that the imiaslavtsy were followers of St. Gregory Palamas by referring to two main points where it claims they differ: 1) St. Gregory never used "God" (*theos*) to refer to both God's energies and his essence; only "divinity" (*theotēs*) can be used in the wider sense. 2) St. Gregory did not confuse an action or energy of God with its result (or its "fruit"). Only words spoken *by* God are his actions; not those with which we speak *about* him. The apostles did hear and see divinity on Tabor, but one does not say that in repeating what they heard to others they were communicating divinity to them. This is where the imiaslavtsy are guilty of divinizing creation – of pantheism.

The Synod's epistle goes on to dismiss all the quotes from scripture where the name of God seems to be equated with God himself as merely examples of a peculiarity of scriptural language. In such cases "the name of God" is simply a "descriptive phrase" as are others like "the ears of the Lord" or the "eyes of the Lord." Just as we do not take the latter literally, so we should not the former.

Though John of Kronstadt does use the disputed phrases, the very fact that no one objected to his language before is evidence that he didn't mean the same thing by it as do Ilarion and Bulatovich. What he was speaking of was subjective, not objective reality – he spoke of what is so only "for us" and "in our consciousness." In order to form no false image of God, while praying we concentrate on the words of the prayer, particularly on God's name; and when God truly makes himself present he does become identified with his name – but this is true only for the one who is praying and during the time of prayer. In any case, Fr. John's words about the power of the name referred not to the name *per se* but to its use in calling upon the Lord. He clearly says that the name will perform no miracles without faith.

As for the effectiveness of sacraments and icons and crosses, this is by no means due to the pronounced or inscribed name of God, nor due to the faith of individuals, but due to the faith of the Church. If the imiaslavtsy's arguments were true, then anyone at all could perform the sacraments – and the church's hierarchy would become superfluous.

In conclusion the name is indeed holy and worthy of worship (*dostopokloniaemo*) because it designates God and was revealed by him, but it is not God himself nor is it even divinity because it is not the divine "energy" but its result. When pronounced with faith it does work miracles, but not of itself, not mechanically or automatically.

Therefore: 1) heads of monasteries are to hold special services (*moleben*s) to pray for the repentance of those who have fallen into error; 2) those who disagree must obey the church and not bother other people; 3) all must forgive one another and stop fighting; 4) *Na Gorakh Kavkaza*, *Apologiia Very*, and all other works written in defense of their doctrines are to be removed from the monasteries and reading them is forbidden; and 5) any who remain stubborn in their beliefs face a church court and possible deprivation of priesthood and/or monastic rank. Now that both the patriarch of Constantinople and the Holy Synod of Russia have spoken, Ilarion and Antonii in particular have no more excuse for holding to their mistaken beliefs and should admit their error and submit to the voice of the Church.

Archbishop Antonii Khrapovitskii's Report

The three reports from which the official epistle was compiled were all printed together in the same issue of *Tserkovnyia Vedomosti*. Each had its own particular emphases. Abp. Antonii's report was devoted mainly to attacking Fr. Antonii Bulatovich. He described his approach to the task of preparing it in a letter to Jerome dated May 14:

Oppressed by a multitude of people and papers, I deliberately secluded myself for four days at the St. Sergius Hermitage near Petersburg in order to compile a refutation of the stupid and ignorant book of Bulatovich, who himself doesn't believe a word of what he cluttered there. This is just such a blackguard (*merzavets*) as Iliodor, who openly repudiated Christ, and I already knew him in 1907 as such. (Pakhomii, 64)[29]

Actually, the report is devoted not so much to refutation as to questioning of motives. Ilarion is said to have dreamed up his new teaching because of vainglory:

> He fell into the so-called "*prelest'* of startsy." Each has his own temptation: for the young it is lust, for the old it is avarice, for bishops it is pride and vainglory, and for startsy – to think up new rules to immortalize their memory in the monastery. ... However, those who, like the starets Ilarion, think up new dogmas to immortalize their memory, sin far more. (872)

In suggesting that the Jesus prayer could replace all others, Ilarion created a temptation for lazy monks and a temptation to laziness for others:

> That's why so many were carried away by the teaching of Ilarion: some by blind zeal and stubbornness, others by laziness, sweetly foretasting that they would soon pass on to that level of perfection where they would not have to stand through church services or read any prayers at all, but just "carry in their heart the name of Jesus." (871)

The lazy were joined by the downright evil:

---

[29]What this refers to is unknown; according to Fr. Antonii the two never even met.

> All that was in our monasticism of disobedience, stubbornness, vainglory, and avarice was taken by this foolish dogma, and without a second thought rejoiced in the opportunity to reject authority and slander the higher powers, to grab the position of leadership, and to pilfer from the monastery bank. (872)

Nevertheless, at least Ilarion may have been sincere; that can hardly be said of Ieroskhimonakh Antonii. Proof that the latter does not even believe what he himself is saying is to be found in his accusations that those who disagree with him are heretics who deny that Jesus Christ is God, who deny the importance of the Jesus prayer and all prayer in general, and who have no true spiritual experience:

> To this we answer that we do confess the divinity of Jesus Christ, and we do highly esteem the Jesus prayer; and we do not pride ourselves in learning but we do place it lower than spiritual experience. However in the book of schema-monk Ilarion we don't see any spiritual experience but rather self-deceptive dreaming. Still less spiritual experience do we find in the book of Bulatovich; there we see only logomachy, i.e. scholasticism, without hard logic and without knowledge of the Bible. (871)

Regardless of what one may think about Bulatovich's logic, he at least never stooped to anything remotely approaching the kind of mud-slinging that pervades Abp. Antonii Khrapovitsky's writings. Here the slanderous accusations flying so free and easy actually constitute the main theme of the archbishop's report, which abounds in phrases like "absurd heresy," "fallen into *prelest*'," "ravings of lunatics" (*bred sumasshedshikh*), "absurdity," "stupidity," "mindless conclusions," and the like. And if he didn't always use the term "heresy," *Novoe Vremia* reported the reason why:

Abp. Antonii of Volynia goes even farther and says that to call this false teaching a heresy is to give it greater honor, since it is simply khlystic idiotic ravings. (May 17:5)

The archbishop even specifies Fr. Antonii's insidious ulterior motives:

> Himself not believing what he is writing, but only wanting to have for himself a means for rebellion in the Athonite monasteries ... this imitator of the new false teaching much more skillfully disseminates it than its originator, for he far exceeds him in cunning and in ability to deceive and intimidate simple-minded Russian monks. (873) Alas, it is necessary to accept the thought that specifically these fights and expulsions [at St. Andrew's] constituted the goal of Fr. Bulatovich in the compiling of his hypocritical (*fal'shivoi*) book, full of obvious perversions of the sacred words and deliberately false interpretations of them. (876)

The report does, however, occasionally depart from *ad hominem* rhetoric to attempt a refutation of arguments made in *Apologiia*, and one must at least give the archbishop credit for having read the book first this time. He says Fr. Antonii's position is based on two main fallacies, of which the first is a false understanding of "name." A name is only a word consisting simply of letters and sounds; its "essence" is not even its meaning but "the movement of air and its striking against our eardrum." Fr. Antonii's claim that "the name of God" means something other than letters and sounds is totally unacceptable:

> And does he even want to say something or simply to obfuscate, to darken the thought of [his] trusting disciple, so that he, having read these lines, would say, "Well, thank God, here they're divinizing neither letters nor sounds, but something different, which I can't understand." Yes – and no one can understand, we will add, because it is impossible to understand nonsense. (878)

Bulatovich's other fundamental error is in not differentiating God's energy or action from what it produces:

> And such absurdity Fr. Bulatovich asserts without any shame; he says that every word spoken on Tabor is God: does that mean both the word "listen" and the word "him" are God? ... the Lord ... denounced the contemporary Jews, saying to them: "serpent, viper's brood." Does that mean that a serpent is God and a viper is God? According to Bulatovich this is definitely so; doubly so, since God created the serpent and the hedgehog and the rabbit they are actions of divinity – are all these wild animals consequently also God? (877)

As for Bulatovich's quotations from scripture and fathers, he consistently perverts their meaning, mainly through a literal understanding of expressions meant metaphorically. This kind of word usage is found throughout the Old Testament and consequently in liturgical and patristic texts as well, including St. Gregory of Sinai's "prayer is God working all in all":

> This is a poetical expression, which replaces other predicates with the word "is": is caused, is sustained, attains, etc. A similar turn of phrase is constantly found in Church poetry: "Jesus most wonderful, amazement of Angels, Jesus most glorious, strengthening of kings, chastity of virgins." From this can we say that the chastity of the righteous is not a quality of soul, undergirded by grace, but rather God himself? (881)

As for the suggestion that the name of God is ultimately the Son of God, the archbishop (blissfully ignorant of the text of St. Maximus) proclaims that, "of course, nowhere is such stupidity said" (875).

Archbishop Nikon Rozhdestvenskii's Report

Abp. Nikon's report placed less emphasis on character assassination and more on reason and logic. A "name" is nothing more than "a conventional sign necessary for our mind, clothed by us in sounds, ... in letters (written), or only represented abstractly, subjectively thought – but in reality not existing outside of our mind (an idea)." (854) Nikon stresses that any word, and a name in particular, has no real existence. So this fact in itself proves illogical the contention that "God's name is God himself," for an unreal name cannot be the very real personal God; an abstract idea cannot be a concrete person. Nor can God or his grace even be present in something that doesn't even exist. Fr. Antonii's main error is precisely here – in speaking of the name as something that has real existence.

Since the imiaslavtsy can't prove their position true logically, they resort to mysticism (a bad thing roughly equivalent to magic in the eyes of the archbishop) and myriads of quotations from various authorities. But the only "authority" who really seems to support their position is John of Kronstadt, who didn't mean what they mean, was not a theologian, and was not attempting to write an accurate exposition of theology in the works they quote. It is of great significance to Nikon that for all their effort the imiaslavtsy were not able to find other quotes from church fathers plainly supporting their position. If this "dogma" were really so important, wouldn't one find irrefutable evidence for it everywhere? He also emphasizes that the name does nothing except through faith and God's good will, then observes that many other holy objects work miracles in the same way – icons, the Lord's garments in the Gospel, relics of saints, etc. Yet we never say that an icon "is God himself" – and an icon is a real object, whereas a name doesn't even really exist. Even in the case of the Church's greatest sacrament – we say the bread and the wine are truly the body and blood of the Lord, but we go no further; we do not say that they "are God himself."

Professor Sergei Troitskii's Report

The last report, Prof. Troitskii's, was obviously the result of much greater investigation and research than the others and even included a historical introduction. Considering the first edition of *Na Gorakh Kavkaza* apart from later developments, Troitskii sees nothing wrong with it other than "certain unfortunate and inexact expressions." Ilarion's error came in the move from simple description of spiritual experience to propounding metaphysical theories, and this was actually caused by Khrisanf's review:

> In this way a practical question about how one should pray becomes with the reviewer a theoretical question about the relationship of God's name to [his] essence. The author followed the reviewer's example. (887)

And controversy grew because of Abp. Antonii's journal:

> When Khrisanf's review, at first, apparently, known only to Fr. Ilarion, appeared in *Russkii Inok*, the arguments about the name "Jesus" passed over from a small circle into the midst of all the Russian monks of Athos, [and] a new phase in the history of the controversy began. (888)

Among the defenders of Ilarion one can now differentiate two main groups: simple uneducated monks who have simply divinized particular combinations of letters and sounds, and educated ones who have developed more sophisticated philosophical and theological theories. The magical and mechanistic views of the former are so obviously contrary to

Christian teaching as to need no refutation, but something similar in a "somewhat softened form" can be found even among the latter, whose main spokesman is Fr. Antonii. This view can thus be considered common to all of them. To show this, Troitskii first concedes that Bulatovich specifically denies ascribing divinity to mere letters and sounds, and then after quoting that section of *Apologiia* adds:

> ... in addition the author announces, "nevertheless, we believe that even to these sounds and letters is attached the grace of God for the sake of the divine name pronounced with them ... Even if you unconsciously invoke the name of the Lord Jesus," he writes, "then you will still have him in his name." And so [Troitskii concludes,] the grace, the power of God is attached to the very sounds and letters of the divine names, irrespective of the thought united with them, and that means one need only pronounce these sounds, pronounce the names of God, and the grace or power united with them will operate by itself, *ex opere operato*. (891)

The fallacy in Troitskii's interpretation is that to whatever degree one can speak of an "unconscious action," to the same degree one can also speak of unconscious thought. As Fr. Antonii says in this very passage, grace is present in the letters and sounds precisely because of the divine name expressed by them, precisely because of their meaning, not "irrespective" of it. As for charges that this view constitutes a belief in magic or in effectiveness *ex opere operato*, Fr. Antonii's understanding of God's presence in his name can be compared to the physical presence of one's human friend, who may choose sometimes to answer the way expected, other times to say nothing at all, and yet other times to say something quite unexpected – yet the person is nevertheless truly present whatever he chooses to do.

Next, Troitskii turns his attention specifically to those who have dreamed up "sophisticated philosophical theories." To counter their claims to be followers of St. Gregory Palamas he offers the same two arguments made by Nikon and Antonii, beginning with the claim that "God" can only mean God's "essence." While acknowledging that the Palamites themselves did use "God" in the wider sense, he argues that they did so rarely and for special reasons no longer valid:

> ... in *Apologiia* it is made clear that in the present case the word "God" is used not in the particular narrow sense of God's essence, but rather in the same wide sense used by the Palamites, in the sense of opposition to all that is created, and in that understanding of opposition, as the Palamites correctly taught, is included not only God's essence but also his energy. But if the Palamites had good reason to use the word "God" not in the usual narrow sense but in the wide sense to expose the heresy of Barlaam, who taught about the createdness of the manifestation of God's energy – the light of Tabor – yet the imiaslavtsy have no right to this. For now no one holds that God's name, as a part of revelation, is a created thing, and consequently they are introducing confusion, giving cause to think that they are identifying God's action with his essence. (893)

The better word for the wider meaning is "divinity," and that is the word used by the councils that affirmed the Palamite teaching. Granted, this is really just an issue of semantics; but then such issues are also important:

> In this way the imiaslavtsy, at least by their terminology, completely stand on the side not of the Palamites, but of the Barlaamites. But it is impossible to consider this heretical terminology a matter of little importance, for the Church worked out the form of its dogmas with long effort, and the formulations established by it have obligatory significance for all who wish to

remain in it, and they serve as a guarantee of unity of thought among church society. (895)

Troitskii's reasoning here – as throughout his report – is both confused and fallacious. It is true that causing dissension by using language easily misunderstood is certainly to be avoided if possible, and presumably would be subject to disciplinary action if continued in defiance of church authorities. However, this was certainly not the case with the imiaslavtsy, who were clearly not motivated by a desire to cause trouble (Abp. Antonii's accusations notwithstanding). They did defy the instructions of Patr. Germanos, but the latter condemned not their terminology but the content of what he thought they believed, and they were contending that he had misunderstood and/or misrepresented their position.

Moreover, saying that the imiaslavtsy stood on the side of Barlaam "by their terminology" is a rather extreme sophism. Troitskii argued that this was so because Barlaam only acknowledged a distinction between "God" and "creation" while St. Gregory added the third category of "divine energies." But this is a gross misrepresentation of what the latter meant to say; his terminology of "essence" and "energies" could have been applied in a similar way to human beings, to animals, even to stones. We know a person by the things he has done, by the things he has said, by what he looks like, by what he habitually does, etc.; yet no matter how well we know the person there remains something beyond our knowledge – the very essence of the person, which is ultimately unknowable and indescribable. Yet in spite of that "limitation" we nevertheless do truly know the person himself through a variety of forms of contact. To equate the person only with that "essence" which always remains beyond our knowledge is to deny that we can know the person at all. The same can be said of our relationship with God. Were Troitskii's position correct the whole of Christian literature would have to be rewritten. One could never know God himself nor describe him in any way. One could not say God is love, for that is one of his characteristics, not his essence. One could not say God is merciful, for that is one of his characteristics, not his essence. One could not say that God heals the sick, for that is the work of his energies. One could not say that God will raise the dead to eternal life, for that is the work of his energies. One could not even say that God as the "unknowable essence" is known or reveals itself in these ways through the energies – for Fr. Antonii's equivalent statement that "the energies name the unnameable essence" Troitskii rejects as an "impossible contradiction." So it is Troitskii's terminology (shared by all three of the Synod's "reporters") that for Christianity is nonsense. What he did with "essence" and "energy" in God was the same as what Nestorius did with "two natures" in Christ, i.e. instead of distinguishing that which is united, he separated them – even while emphasizing their inseparability.

Troitskii does concede that "name" is sometimes used by scripture in a way that can be equated with the technical term "energy," a concession neither of the other reports make:

> The name of God, understood in the sense of God's revelation and at the same time from its objective side, i.e. in the sense of *the revealing* of truths to man, is the eternal, inseparable-from-God energy of God, received by people only insofar as their createdness, limitedness, and moral dignity allows. To the word "name" used in this sense is applied the appellation divinity, but not God, insofar as "God is the act-or" (*deistvuiushchii*), and not the action, and insofar as "God is above divinity." (906-7)

Beyond word usage, Troitskii sees the error of the imiaslavtsy to be in confusing the objective with the subjective. He believes that when they say "the name of God is God," they mean by "name" the human act of pronouncing it rather than the objective side of divine revelation. And speaking of the name as "the very idea of God" or the thought of God is no better, for that too is a human action, not a divine one. He accuses them of claiming that the human understanding of God can be "adequate" to him, though it is impossible that the finite can fully comprehend the infinite. This is a misrepresentation; no imyaslavets ever called God's name God himself in the sense of absolute identification, and Fr. Antonii in *Apologiia* specifically and repeatedly denied that the divine name is "adequate" or all-inclusive.

Invocation of the name in prayer is yet another issue. Here Troitskii acknowledges a reciprocal action of both God and man:

> But if prayer is always not only the action of God's grace, but also of our spirit, then to call prayer God means to call God even the action of a created, limited spirit, while the Church doesn't call God even God's action, but calls it only divine. (897)

St. Gregory of Sinai's phrase is therefore explained not by ascribing it to poetic language as does Abp. Antonii, but by saying that St. Gregory was speaking only of the "objective side" of prayer.

In conclusion Troitskii points to a variety of sometimes contradictory positions in various writings of the imiaslavtsy and suggests that they themselves have yet to fully define what they believe. But in general one can summarize that they are wrong both in terminology (including energies in "God himself") and in content (confusing the objective side of divine revelation with the subjective).[30] Troitskii's analysis of confusion on the side of the imiaslavtsy is a fair one; having been pushed into a defensive position by Khrisanf's review, many monks a good deal less capable than Fr. Antonii Bulatovich had also taken pen in hand. And under that pressure some of them probably did use imprecise phraseology that could be misinterpreted. But a careful, unbiased attempt to understand their main points could have avoided such misinterpretations. Unfortunately, not one of the Synod's reporters seems to have been motivated by a desire to understand so much as by a desire to find bases for condemnation. Some reasons why Abp. Antonii took this approach have already been presented. Not enough information about the other two is available today to make a similar analysis of their motives. One may nevertheless reasonably suppose that for Troitskii the power and influence of the archbishop from Volynia was not without effect, and that for Nikon personal friendship with a fellow member of the Synod and/or political camaraderie played a role.

Many greeted the Synod's decision as the final word that would terminate the conflict once and for all. That was to prove a vain hope, and it was with the foresight of a Neville Chamberlain that one *Novoe Vremia* reporter entitled his May 16 article about it "An End to the Matter of Bulatovich."

---

[30]This last issue will be dealt with in ch. 7 below.

6
Manu Militari

Archbishop Nikon's Trip to Athos

Even before formally reaching its decision, the Holy Synod had requested and received permission from Patr. Germanos to send Abp. Nikon on a mission to Athos. Troitskii was to accompany him, and their official goal was "to act upon the Russian monks ... in the sense of peace-making and subjecting them to church authority regarding the question of God's name." (*Terkovnyi Vestnik* 1913 21:641) Detailed information about the course of the mission is available in the official reports of these two, but the reliability of that information is open to question. Both reports were compiled afterward in the midst of a great public outcry against the expedition's outcome, so a concern for self-justification will have made it desirable for the reporters to present the imiaslavtsy in as bad a light as possible.

Nikon left St. Petersburg on May 23/June 5. After stopping in Kiev to pick up Vice-Consul Shcherbina he proceeded to Odessa. There he was joined by Troitskii and began his work by making speeches in churches at local dependencies of Athonite monasteries which were "infected by the heresy." Of these first attempts at persuasion he writes:

> It is noteworthy that all of the speeches of the monks in defense of the false teaching and later on Athos had one and the same character: [all consisted of] fervent declarations that for the name of God they were ready to lay down their soul, suffer, and die (as if we were some kind of torture-masters). When we would tell them that no one was requiring this of them but that things were just being explained to them; that we too all piously honor the name

of God; [that] we acknowledge that it is worthy of praise and is glorious; but that it itself is nevertheless not God himself – then they would begin to get wildly excited and to cry out one and the same phrase "God himself! God himself!" (1504)

As had others before him, Nikon found himself accused of denying the divinity of Jesus Christ himself:

> For my part, no matter how many times I would repeat that I believe and confess that our Lord Jesus Christ is the true God; that the discussion is not about his person but only about words, about his names; that the Lord himself is one thing and his name another – nothing helped. They would already be accusing me that I don't call Jesus Christ God, that I am a heretic. (1504)

The next stop was Constantinople, where he held a brief consultation with the patriarch and picked up two more key personnel: General Consul Shebunin and Secretary of the Embassy Serafimov.

Arriving at the Rossikon on June 4/17 aboard the naval gunboat *Donets*, Abp. Nikon found a cold reception:

> Below, on the dock and near the gates, were gathered about 150 to 200 orthodox[31] monks with their abbot, Archimandrite Misail, at the head. The others either stood at a distance, not wanting to receive a blessing from me, or did not come down from the terraces [and] were simply spectators of this meeting, which, I must admit, seemed to me far from "ceremonious." (1507)

What he does not speak of here is his own coldness – imiaslavtsy later recalled that he himself refused to give his blessing to those of them who requested it. While not mentioning that behavior

---

[31] As opposed to the "heretics," i.e., the imyaslavtsy.

in his report, he does recount asking during his discussion with the patriarch whether or not he should give his blessing to those of the heretics who would ask for it out of a sense of propriety and being told "No."

After a short service in the monastery's main church he began his first speech, though relatively few came to hear it. The emphasis was not on explaining or on dialogue but on the importance of obedience and the consequences of disobedience:

> Not entering into the details of this question, for the time was already late, I asked the listeners to direct special attention to the fact that this question had already been examined thoroughly and in detail by church authority, [and] that it is not the business of monk-simpletons to delve into dogmatic investigations, which are anyway beyond the powers of their minds unprepared by science. Moreover the holy fathers forbid this to monks. And what is most important – to remember the command of the Savior about obedience to the Church and to the divinely established pastors in order not to be subjected to judgment for disobedience and even excommunication from it. (1508)

Nikon spent the night on the *Donets*, and the next day saw the beginning of several weeks of efforts at convincing the intransigent monks of their error.

Nikon and Troitskii held private discussions with the leaders of the "heretics"; they passed out brochures and pamphlets; they read the Synod's epistle publicly in church and followed it with more speeches; Troitskii stationed himself in the library inviting any and all to come and debate with him; and both traveled to New Thebaide and other nearby communities for more discussions. Nikon says he planned also to go to St. Andrew's, but they would only receive him without soldiers, and he did not want to do that because travel was dangerous. Bands of robbers were roaming the Holy Mountain due to Greece's troubles with Bulgaria – one monk even arrived at St. Panteleimon's with a gunshot wound to the hand. So instead of going himself, Nikon directed Troitskii to visit St. Andrew's and the more distant *kellii* (monastic cells).

Their efforts met with much opposition. Nikon describes one fruitless speech in the church of the Pokrov:

> After lunch they rang the bell and the church filled up with monks. After putting on the mantia I went out to the ambo. A tight ring of "imiaslavtsy" surrounded me, but the consul had taken the precaution of placing sailors in front of me. There were rumors that the "imiaslavtsy" were threatening, "Let Nikon fall into their hands and then he'll know what it means to revile the name of God." ... I appealed to common sense, noting that their teacher Bulatovich considers all of the word of God to be God, but after all, there are many human words there, for example the words of the fool "There is no God" ... and about God's creatures, like the worm: What?! Is all this God? The names of God, as words, only designate God, refer to him, but by themselves still are not God: the name "Jesus" is not God, the name "Christ" is not God. At these words, on command of Irenei were heard cries of "Heretic! He teaches that Christ isn't God!" ... they kept on interrupting me with noises and shouts but I finished my reading and explanations anyway. ... [Then Irenei] proudly announced that none of my exhortations would have any success, and the noise of those who agreed with him confirmed his words. They shouted at me "Heretic! Crocodile from the sea! Seven-headed snake! Wolf in sheep's clothing!" (1510-11)

As for the one thousand copies of his report to the synod which he had brought with him to pass out, "they tore it in pieces and threw it to the wind."

Some sense of the difficulty of the task undertaken by Nikon and Troitskii, even with monks who were willing to listen, can be gained from the following story:

> Ieromonakh Flavy, an elder (*dukhovnik*) from the hermitage of Thebaide, came to me five times, now repenting, now denying the orthodox teaching. Finally, I asked Sergei Viktorovich Troitskii to take care of him separately, and he spoke with him for about two hours. But even after this conversation, during which the whole false teaching was thoroughly picked apart, Flavy would only deny the false teaching after, having made several prostrations, he decided to draw lots: To believe, or not to believe the Synod? And by the mercy of God, twice they came up "Believe." Then he came to me and with obvious agitation of soul said, "Now I believe as the Synod has ordered." (1515)

Others were firmer in their convictions and were inclined to defend them vigorously. Nikon reports that some dug up and spread around a text of St. John Chrysostom which they felt to be applicable to heretic-archbishops:

> If you hear someone reviling God on the square or in the crossroads, go up and say something. And if necessary, hit him; don't back off, hit him in the face or box him on the ears, sanctify your hand with the blow ... (1513)

There was a "rebellion" within three days of the expedition's arrival, apparently due to Consul Shebunin's threat to imprison Ireney on the *Donets*. The latter fled to a monastery church, an alarm bell was rung, and masses of his followers converged upon the church in his support, making it impossible to carry out the threat. The consul requested reinforcements. They arrived on June 13/26, and when he ordered the 123 soldiers ashore to take up posts around the monastery there was another moment of tension as the monks gathered at the gate to obstruct their entrance. The soldiers were let through peacefully only after they explained that they were there just to guard the monastery in view of rumors that there were plans to burn it or rob its bank.

On June 29/July 12 the consul decided to verify everyone's passports. This move was said to be inspired by a rumor according to which someone had threatened that "since in this world he had already sent two policemen to the other world, it wouldn't cost him anything to send an abbot there as well." (1515) In the process each monk was asked how he believed, and of about 1,700 in all, a little over 700 proclaimed their nonacceptance of the "heresy"; still a minority, but an increase over the ratio of one fourth estimated at Nikon's arrival.

Nikon's Final Solution

The following day the archbishop proclaimed a three-day fast scheduled for the second, third, and fourth of July, during which petitions for the "uprooting of error" were to be added to litanies in the church services. This was actually not another means for admonition but rather a means for keeping as many monks in the monastery as possible. July 5 is the feast day of the Great Lavra, the senior monastery on Athos, and since the celebration draws masses of monks from all over the Holy Mountain, many had already begun leaving St. Panteleimon's. But Nikon's company had already decided to deport the intransigents, had requested a ship suitable for the task, was expecting its arrival any day, and did not want any imiaslavtsy to miss deportation simply because they were temporarily away.

When the *Kherson* arrived on the second day of the fast, Consul Shebunin did not even wait for the fast's completion. (Or rather Nikon later blamed Shebunin for what followed; it is, however, difficult to believe that the latter acted without the archbishop's knowledge or consent or even direct orders.) Shebunin informed the imiaslavtsy that all who would not sign the required papers expressing acceptance of the Synod's epistle would have to go to the ship. They were not told what was in store for them. They asked for a promise that they would be given a share in the monastery's wealth proportionate to their numbers, but received instead an offer of twenty-five rubles to monks who had lived in the monastery for ten years, fifty rubles for twenty years, and one hundred for thirty. They asked to be given their own monastery in Russia. Shebunin refused. The result was the scene recounted at the beginning of the Introduction.

Much about that scene sounds almost comical, but in fact the official reports do not reflect the true level of violence with which the soldiers, armed with bayonets and joined even by some of the monastery's other monks, attacked the soaked imiaslavtsy. Nikon reported about twenty-five "'injured', i.e., scratched," but it is hardly possible to imagine a bayonet making only a "scratch." The monks themselves later claimed that forty had to be treated in the monastery hospital, four of whom died later from their wounds and were quietly buried that night (see Nivière 350). After the attack, the imiaslavtsy were brought to the boat immediately, and the next day their things – or rather the less desirable portions of them – were brought to them from their cells. But then it was found that some were needed for vital jobs in the monastery – and so they were then forcibly removed from their comrades on the ship and brought back to shore.

On the sixth/nineteenth of July, soldiers were dispatched to St. Andrew's. There the monks chose to avoid a repeat of the St. Panteleimon's affair and agreed to go peacefully, having been given the opportunity to take their things with them. After their departure Jerome staged a triumphant return on July 8/21.

The Deportation

According to the official figures released by the Russian Church, 621 monks were deported aboard the *Kherson* and a week later 212 more aboard the *Chikhachov*. Of the first figure 436 were from St. Panteleimon's and 185 from St. Andrew's; the 212 on the second ship were more monks from the Rossikon who chose to leave voluntarily rather than signing papers repudiating their beliefs. Vechevoy (49) and Bulatovich (*Moia bor'ba*,158, 64) estimate that in the ensuing months as many as one thousand more Russian monks unwilling to sign left Athos on their own. This supposition is indirectly corroborated by the modern historian Smolitsch, who reports that Russian monks on Athos totaled 3,496 in 1910 but only 1,914 in 1914. (305) Subtracting the 833 deportees, that leaves 849 unaccounted for.

While impressive in themselves, these numbers actually belie the true strength of opposition to the Synod's position among the Athonite monks, for many of those who signed did so only to avoid trouble. If 1,000 monks of St. Panteleimon's declared themselves "confessors of the name" on June 29, and only 643 were deported a few days later, that leaves about 350 who rather abruptly decided to sign the necessary papers. After holding firm through a month of constant exhortation to recant, these monks are not likely to have actually changed their beliefs in a matter of days. Fr. Parfeny, in whose cell of the Annunciation Fr. Antonii Bulatovich had lived after leaving St. Andrew's, and who had published locally many of his works, probably typifies their attitude. Nikon recounts:

... he sent to me his representative to sign for all the brethren [of his cell] the repudiation of the heresy. ... I told the representative that he could sign for himself but for the others – no: let them sign themselves. He signed and took with him a sheet to present to the starets and the others. ... About a week went by. On the sixth of July, already after the removal of the heretics from the monastery, the same representative came to me and gave [me] three letters from Parfenii at once. The starets wrote that just as he has learned to believe from the cradle, so he will believe, and repeated nearly the whole symbol of the faith [i.e., the creed] and asked me to leave him to die in peace – but not a word about the synodal epistle, not about the decrees of the patriarchs, not about faith in the name of God. Then I wrote to him decisively and briefly: why is he being deceitful, why does he in not a single letter answer the question: how does he believe about the names of God; and [why does he] not sign the repudiation? I asked that as the starets of a cell where more than 50 brothers live, he answer me, whether yes or no. If yes, then good, but if no, then I will report this to the Holy Synod and the patriarch and – right away tomorrow – to the *Koinotes* ... In the evening on that very day the old man sent me the formula of repudiation with signatures – his and the elder brethren.

It is not difficult to imagine just what depth of conviction those signatures and many others like them expressed.

And the monks' fears concerning the consequences for not signing were not groundless; the lot of those who were expelled was a hard one. On the *Kherson* they found themselves treated as criminals: they were kept locked up and under guard, allowed to walk on deck only infrequently and in small groups, and fed prison rations of shchi (cabbage soup) in the morning and kasha (cooked grain) in the evening. When the ship arrived in Odessa on July 13, police cordoned off the dock to keep the public away, then boarded the ship to interrogate the monks. The latter were presented with forms to sign stating that they had left their monastery voluntarily (!!), retained no claims on it, and were voluntarily removing their monastic clothing. A complaint they made later notes also that these forms were presented as being nothing more than verification of identity – and since many of the monks were illiterate they could not tell otherwise. Before being taken ashore their things (books, icons, clothing, money – everything) were taken from them by customs agents. Then they were variously led or driven to jail, the police station, or St. Andrew's dependency in Odessa.

To the latter only eight were sent, whose monastic rank the Holy Synod recognized; the rest were treated as if they had never been tonsured. For justification of its treatment of them the Synod referred to an 1836 decision according to which all monks coming to Russia but tonsured outside of it were required to go through a three-year trial period before their monastic rank would be recognized. The regulation was certainly not intended as a simple way to defrock monks without having to bother with a church court – but that is precisely how it was used. After jail stays varying from two to fifty days their monastic clothing was forcibly removed; they were given "identical 4.5 ruble costumes" of lay clothing; their hair was cut;[32] and they were sent "home" as private citizens, presumably to whatever part of the country where it was determined that they had relatives. Reportedly forty who were suspected of being criminals or whose identity could not be confirmed were kept in jail indefinitely. The monks were not given back either their possessions taken by customs or their

---

[32] Athonite monks prefer to let their hair and beard grow long, rarely if ever cutting them.

money, though the police promised to send the latter on to them later. Many never saw it again or only got part of it back.

The shock and hardship endured in all this by the monks may seem obvious but must be incomprehensible for anyone not familiar with monastic life. Many had lived as monks for twenty or thirty years or more, during which time their whole life revolved around church services often totaling eight hours or more each day. The suffering for those who suddenly had that focus of their life removed from them and a return to it forbidden is hardly imaginable for a modern American except perhaps to compare it to the death of a spouse.

Besides that, many would have had no work responsibilities in the monastery; aside from worship services they would have attended only to their private rule of prayer, which could occupy many additional hours every day. Others might have had some relatively short and simple daily work assignment (such as sweeping floors, setting and clearing tables, etc.), usually involving few hours and little if any pressure for production and efficiency. Such people would have no salable skills "in the world" and if they did would not be desirable laborers. After years of "work" done primarily as a necessary break from the far more important mental work of prayer, they would have neither ability nor inclination to suddenly become productive hirelings working hard, long hours every day. To set such people loose to fend for themselves in a capitalistic society lacking a developed social welfare system was cruel almost beyond belief. Small wonder that a few later regretted choosing not to sign the repudiation,[33] as did one who wrote to friends on Athos that

---

[33]Although as late as September *Novoe Vremia* reported that only "10 of 600" monks recanted. (Sep. 4:5)

"when the police officers took off of me my monastic clothing and put on me a jacket and a cap, I cried bitterly." (Pakhomy, 208)

Nor was the lot of those few whose monasticism was recognized an easy one. More than a month after his arrival in Odessa, Archimandrite David wrote to a newspaper complaining of the "strict regime" he had to undergo at St. Andrew's dependency there. The abbot was openly calling him and his companions "deluded heretics, antichrists, deprived of communion and monasticism, and excommunicated from the church," and he made life difficult for them in other ways as well:

> At the beginning when we moved into the monastery they gave us food from the brotherhood's kitchen, and, although rarely and with difficulty, brothers were permitted to come to us. But now it is already the third week that no one is permitted to come to us and we are not permitted to go anywhere. Now they give us our food from the brothers' leftovers and the visitors' kitchen. Borshch and soup they pour into one container; kasha, stew, boiled potatoes, macaroni, and other things they throw together in another. The food is repulsive. (NV 1913 Aug 24:13)

Response to Nikon's Final Solution

The outcry in the Russian press against Abp. Nikon's handling of the affair was nearly universal. Troitskii himself later wrote that only Skvortsov's *Kolokol* and an insignificant Odessa paper expressed approval. Some condemned the use of force against the monks for political reasons, regretting that the loss of a Russian majority on Athos would mean the demise of Russia's plan for internationalizing Athos instead of giving the peninsula to Greece. Some suggested the Greeks had deliberately used the controversy precisely for that purpose. And some raised questions about the legality of the move, insofar as Athos was not Russian territory and many of the monks were no longer even Russian citizens. But most simply deplored the use of military force as a means for settling a theological dispute, as did *Moskovskiia Vedomosti* on July 28 in a front-page article:

> The first time, we heard about violence and fights occurring among private persons. While that was not good and not Christian, it was a private matter. But now appears before us the church authority, a representative of the Holy Synod. ... this is no longer a simple brawl of the monks themselves, who have no worldly or spiritual authority. This is much worse.

Novoe Vremia asked, "Who gave the order to take such a measure? Really the archbishop? And does monastic or in general ecclesiastical law foresee such a punishment as a cold shower?" (Aug. 22:3) The Moscow paper *Russkiia Vedomosti* (Russian News) printed a vehement article comparing the events on Athos to the burnings of old-believer monasteries in the 1830's and lamenting that "this brings us back to the era of Nicholas." (Sep. 4:3)

Adding their voices to the clamor were several famous Russian theologians. Nicholas Berdyaev (1874-1948), who had once been exiled for socialist activities, found himself in trouble with the government again when he attacked in print this misuse of state power. In his autobiography he recounts his reasons for writing *Gasiteli Dukha* (Quenchers of the Spirit) and the results:

I didn't have special sympathies for imyaslavstvo, but violence in spiritual life and the meanness and unspirituality of the Holy Synod upset me. The issue of the newspaper in which the article was printed was confiscated, and I was placed under judgment according to an statute on blasphemy, the punishment for which was eternal exile in Siberia. My lawyer thought my case hopeless. (*Samopoznanie*, 219)

Berdyaev was saved first by the onset of World War I, which delayed his case, and then by the revolution, which made blasphemy rewardable rather than punishable.

Another well-known theologian, Sergius Bulgakov (1871-1944), similarly deplored Nikon's actions. In the September issue of *Russkaia Mysl'* (Russian Thought) he wrote:

> The color of shame, of indignation, of sorrow, [and] of insult for the church appears on one's face at the thought of this expedition and of that sad role which an orthodox archbishop permitted himself, not refraining from moral participation in the foul treatment of the Athonite monks. (42)

This was only mentioned in passing, however; the article focused rather on the issue of how "dogmas" are determined to be true or false in the Orthodox Church – and how the Holy Synod's behavior constituted a betrayal of the very nature of the Church.

Bulgakov observed that settling such disputes is no problem for the Roman Catholic Church thanks to its doctrine of papal infallibility and its dividing the Church into "teaching church" and "taught church." Even though not every papal statement is called infallible, such doctrines reflect a view according to which the church hierarchy of itself decides dogmatic questions while the "laity" must simply accept and obey. For the orthodox things are not so simple:

Manu Militari 147

> The same question is posed completely otherwise in orthodoxy. There is no external dogmatic authority in orthodoxy. Such are not the organs of higher church administration or hierarchy, nor even the so-called "ecumenical councils" themselves, which, in essence, only proclaimed and confirmed a dogma which had been received rather by the whole body of the Church. ... [Quoting A. S. Khomiakov:] "In the true Church there is no teaching Church. The *whole* Church teaches; in other words, the Church in its wholeness. The Church does not acknowledge a teaching Church in a different sense." (38)

Since truth in the Orthodox Church is preserved by all of its members and not just by the hierarchy, conciliarity is of the utmost importance. Dogmatic questions are to be resolved preeminently at councils attended by both hierarchs and others, all of whom then merely witness to an already existing common consciousness.

Only that which has already been received by the whole church may be proclaimed a dogma,

> ... and even the higher hierarchy may not appropriate this right to itself, being authorized ... to condemn only those opinions which constitute in themselves direct or indirect contradiction of already acknowledged dogmas, and which are in this sense obviously heretical. But in new questions, posed for the first time in church-historical evolution – up until dogmatic maturity sets in for one or another teaching and it is fixed in the church's consciousness there remains freedom for personal investigation, for that which is technically called sometimes "theological opinions" (in contradistinction to dogmas). (40)[34]

---

[34] Specific examples of what this means: "On essentially such a position many thinkers lived in orthodoxy and unhypocritically considered themselves faithful to it, such as Bukharev, Dostoyevsky with his chiliastic hopes, V. S.

This freedom of investigation constitutes the "living nerve of the Church," and to stifle it is to "quench the spirit." It always involves the danger of heresy, but heresy itself is possible only in the presence of "dogmatic life," as scripture itself affirms: "It is necessary that heresies be among you so that the approved ones may become manifest ..." (1 Cor 11:19)

"Reasoning theoretically," a heresy can be in two directions: thought or will. The first occurs when a "theological opinion" obviously contradicts an already received dogma. The second occurs when someone calls their "theological opinion" – regardless of its content – obligatory for all and begins to call others who do not accept it heretics. In the second case "even a true opinion, if it becomes a means for church division and creates a will toward it, can obtain a heretical shade." (43)

The point of all this is that no one in the debate about God's name acted according to these basic tenets of Orthodoxy. To some degree the Athonite monks erred by ascribing obligatory value to their "theological opinion," but by far the greatest blame lies on the hierarchy. If the essence of the new teaching truly consisted only in a mechanistic and magical divinization of letters and sounds, then the response of church authorities would have been correct, but in fact the issues are not nearly so clear and even now there is neither unanimity nor even a clear understanding of them in "church circles." The question is rather both highly complex and of fundamental importance. Ultimately it is about "a theory of prayer, how to understand the

---

Soloviev with his teaching about Sofia, N. F. Fedorov with his teaching about the resurrection, Tyutchev, A. Tolstoy, K. Leontiev, ..." (40)

real effectiveness of prayer, in which to the invocation of God's name, and therefore to God's name itself, belongs primary significance." (41)

The authorities should have begun by encouraging debate to clarify the issues. Bulgakov suggests that Patr. Germanos did not do so because of "national-political motives" and that his condemnation, which proceeded "with highly suspicious speed and lightness" was specifically intended to give the Greeks the canonical right to expel large numbers of Russians from Athos and thereby put themselves in the majority once again. (Such analyses of the patriarch's motives were common in the Russian press.)

The Russian Holy Synod did no better. Noting a complete absence of the issue from all of the theological academies' journals, Bulgakov assumes the Synod began by resorting to "the beloved method of shutting mouths." And having cut off initial debate, it then made three poor choices of people to advise it by submitting reports. Abp. Antonii was obviously prejudiced, Nikon had only a seminary education, and Troitskii was an "up to now unknown" professor, a "gutta-perchalike theologian,[35] convenient also for his portability" (44).[36] Bulgakov asks:

> ... why were the spiritual academies and representatives of the orthodox pastorate and laity not consulted, in general why was at least an external decorum of "conciliarity" not observed – to this there can be no satisfactory answer. (44)

---

[35]"Rubbery," i.e., flexible; apparently referring to a willingness to tailor theological conclusions to the desires of superiors.

[36]Referring to the Synod's sending him to Athos along with Nikon.

Furthermore even the three reports were not unanimous, varying from the "extreme rationalism" of Abp. Antonii to the obscure position "approaching 'imyaslavstvo'" of Troitskii. Yet even if all three had been formulated well and were unanimous, the decision would carry no absolute authority, "no matter how much our synod tries to copy the pope."

The mission to Athos manifested the same wrong attitude:

> Abp. Nikon did not consider it necessary to visit Athos and hear out the Athonite "confessors" while still compiling his report to the synod, when it would have been possible to freely exchange opinions. He appeared there rather with a prepared sentence and a request of obedience under threat of excommunication and ... expulsion, and in spite of that he complains that he was met coldly and mistrustfully (43; ellipsis the author's).

The same point about the archbishop's attitude had been made by Fr. Antonii (NV July 25:5), who also observed that by choosing to keep his living quarters on the *Donets* rather than in the monastery itself Nikon had made himself inaccessible to most of the monks who desired to speak with him.

Nevertheless, Bulgakov concludes that the Athonite affair essentially constitutes a "joyful event in the life of the Church" because it proves the "vitality of orthodoxy," which is still able as it was in the past to beget martyrs and confessors for the faith. And this is not the end of the debate but rather a "prologue to further dogmatic movement" in which all members of the church must take part.

Fr. Florensky, apparently less reluctant to take sides, wrote an article entitled "Archbishop Nikon: Spreader of 'Heresy'" (see Andronik 287). He still thought it wiser not to do so openly, however; when published both in an anthology edited by Fr.

Antonii Bulatovich and separately in pamphlet form, the work was unsigned. How much influence it or its author had on the controversy is difficult to say.[37]

Criticism of the Russian church's behavior came even from the other Orthodox churches. Less than a week after the exiles arrived in Odessa, the patriarchs of Constantinople, Jerusalem, and Alexandria joined in submitting a formal protest to the Holy Synod regarding its non-recognition of the monks' monastic rank merely on the basis of their tonsure outside of Russia. Although the text of that protest was never published, *Russkiia Vedomosti* (July 21:3) reported that the patriarchs expressed concern about the "belittling of the prestige of autocephalous eastern-patriarchal church[es]."

Rumors that some members of the Synod itself were also dissatisfied with the turn of events on Athos were rampant. *Novoe Vremia* reported:

> We are told that all of what occurred on Athos happened, supposedly, without the Synod's knowledge and that it had to contend with an already established fact. So then, in order not to injure the prestige of a Russian archbishop and emissary of the Synod, it became necessary to sanction the measures taken by him. (July 27:4)

Others said some of the hierarchs on the Synod felt that force had not really been necessary, that Nikon had overreacted and

---

[37]Another churchman speaking out on the side of the imyaslavtsy was Vladimir Franzevich Ern (1882-1915). However, his main efforts on their behalf consisted only in a few magazine articles and a short pamphlet, and they were not published until 1916 and 1917. See the Bibliography.

behaved tactlessly, and even that he should be removed from his synodal post.

Nikon's and Troitskii's Defense

Such universal opposition gave the deported monks hopes that the Synod might change its stand, so they submitted a formal petition for reconsideration. But before it could be acted upon, Nikon's and Troitskii's reports had to be heard, and they were largely devoted to justifying the actions taken on Athos. Nikon claimed that through their violent behavior the imiaslavtsy had made their own expulsion inevitable. That so many Athonite monks should be of such poor character he attributed to the rapid growth of the Russian population on the Holy Mountain and to poor controls in Russia over who could go there. Noting that even military deserters and political exiles found it a safe haven, he asserted:

> ... among them appeared people who were seeking not so much spiritual asceticism as the satisfaction of their personal vainglory, a particular careerism, a searching for a certain preeminence among the others – I would say – "diotrefism." Bulatovich is typical of such monks. Not having at the base of their spiritual upbringing real ecclesiality, such people can easily give in to temptations to depart to the side, away from the teaching of the Church, from the spirit of its traditions ... (1520)

As for the violence of July 3, he emphasized that he played no direct role, that he did not even witness it, and that it was the responsibility of the civil authorities. This is a rather lame excuse, however. As *Moskovskiia Vedomosti* charged after hearing it; if the church and state authorities had acted so independently, there should also have been a report to the Synod from the latter. In any case the civil authorities would have done nothing without Abp. Nikon's approval and/or direct orders.

Troitskii presented a variety of practical reasons for the expulsions. He acknowledges concerns that bringing the "heretics" back and resettling them all over Russia would merely infect the homeland with what was once a strictly Athonite plague. But he argues that Athos is too important to the Orthodox world to leave heretics there; they would have eventually corrupted all of Russian Athos; and then they would have used the tremendous financial and organizational resources of the great Athonite monasteries to spread their heresy in Russia itself anyway. Not only that, but they would have had the advantage of the aura of authority that belongs to the name of Athos among Orthodox faithful. But now, on the other hand, they have no such means at their disposal and not even the spiritual authority of being monks thanks to their having been defrocked – so the amount of damage they can do is actually much less.

The option of resettling them in dependencies of the Athonite monasteries located outside of Russia had been considered. But this was rejected by the embassy in Constantinople, which didn't want to have to deal with the attendant problems. Also, it would have been difficult to do that resettling within a foreign country, it would have been difficult to prevent their return to Athos, and they would have been able to continue their propaganda.

Troitskii also argues that if the Russians hadn't taken action as they did, the Greeks would have. This was to be avoided for several reasons: it would have been an indirect acknowledgement of Greek authority over Athos;[38] the Greeks would have done it with cruelties and plundering; and they would have tried to remove as many Russians as possible in order to diminish Russian influence on Athos. "In general, to leave thousands of Russian citizens and millions in Russian money to the whims of the Greeks would have been extremely careless." (OIB 174) As for the expulsion's effect on Russian prestige there vis-a-vis the Greeks, the loss of such troublemakers couldn't possibly hurt. And in any case the overpopulation at St. Panteleimon's was alleviated.

Whether for these or other reasons, the members of the Synod were not inclined to condemn Nikon's actions. They did remain divided over whether to employ more repressive measures or treat the exiled monks mercifully, but at a crucial meeting on August 27 those who supported the latter course of action were absent.[39] Hence the resulting decision (*opredelenie*) approved of Nikon's actions and specified a series of further measures to be taken against the imiaslavtsy. Their petition for a church court was to be ignored, but since they were actually under the jurisdiction of the patriarch of Constantinople, the Synod would ask him to hold one. It would also ask him for permission to receive back into communion those who would repent.

Meanwhile the monks were to be officially renamed *imiabozhniki* ("name-god-niks" or "name divinizers"); clergy of the areas to which they had been sent were to be warned of their presence and told to admonish them and take steps against their

---

[38] Athos' political fate had not yet been decided; it was at the time under Greek "occupation" rather than Greek "sovereignty".

[39] Innocent, Exarch of Georgia and Aleksey of Tobol'sk. *Rech'* Aug 29:4.

propaganda; and lists of names were to be distributed to all monasteries warning them not to take in any of the exiled monks except those willing to repent. For the latter a form was provided which they would have to sign wherein they would admit to having fallen into "heretical thinking" (*mudrovanie*); avow acceptance of the epistles of Joachim, Germanos, and the Synod; reject the teaching found in *Na Gorakh Kavkaza* and *Apologiia*; and acknowledge that "all names of God are to be honored relatively and not divinely (*bogolepno*)" and are "by no means to be considered God himself."

The next step was to aid the Russian pastors in their work of admonition by undertaking a thorough theological exposé of the heresy. That task was entrusted to Professor Troitskii.

7
The Pen Supplements the Sword

Immediately upon returning to St. Petersburg, Mr. Troitskii began writing theological critiques of the new heresy. Individual articles were published by the Holy Synod in pamphlet form, one appeared in Skvortsov's *Missionerskoe Obozrenie*, and a long series designed to serve as a comprehensive refutation of every aspect of the heretical teaching found its way into the Synod's journal *Tserkovnyia Vedomosti*. That series and a few other articles Troitskii then combined into the book *Ob imenakh Bozhiikh i imiabozhnikakh* (About the names of God and the imiabozhniki), which was published immediately by the Holy Synod.

One chapter of this book reprinted an article entitled "Was Fr. John Sergiev (of Kronstadt) an imyabozhnik?" While Troitskii reminds the reader that even saints are fallible and that Fr. John in particular has not even been canonized, his main point is not that Fr. John erred, but that he didn't mean the disputed phrase the way the imiabozhniki mean it:

> After all, the word "is" is used also in the sense: "designates," "depicts." Imagine to yourself that on a well hangs a picture depicting St. Panteleimon's monastery. Now, if a person unfamiliar with it asks "What is that?" then of course he will get the answer "This is St. Panteleimon's monastery"; and in this answer the word "is" replaces the word "designates," "depicts." "By incorrect word usage," says St. Gregory of Nyssa, "we call a likeness a person, but particularly we call the living essence by this word." And so in what sense in this expression of Fr. John's, "the name of the Lord is the Lord himself," is the word "is" used – the particular sense or the sense of replacing the word "depicts"? (155)

This is begging the question, for the whole controversy is precisely about the relationship between designating and being. Troitskii takes it for granted that the two concepts are radically different and mutually exclusive, and since he can show that Fr. John did use "is" to mean "designates," he feels that that in itself proves his point.

This basic theme he develops at length in the main section of his book. There he attempts to draw a parallel between the controversy that arose over *Na Gorakh Kavkaza* and a fourth-century one between St. Gregory of Nyssa and the Arian Eunomius. Eunomius believed that the divine names express the very "nature" or "essence" of God, and so he based his denial of Jesus Christ's divinity on the argument that since the name "Unbegotten" expresses God's true nature, the "begotten" Son could not share that nature. Hence Jesus Christ as the Son of God could not be God. St. Gregory refuted this by explaining – as did St. Gregory Palamas a thousand years later – that God's names express not his essence but his "energies" and his characteristics; not what he is, but what he has done or what he does or what he is like. The names answer the question "who," not "what" is God. So any and all names describe him inadequately, not absolutely; he is in one sense nameable and in another above and beyond any name. In the sense Eunomius meant there is in fact no possible name for God. Therefore the Father's being "unbegotten" does not exclude the "begotten" Son from sharing his nature and consequently being truly God himself.

To tie this aspect of Eunomius's teaching to the imiaslavtsy Troitskii quoted the following from Ilarion's response to Khrisanf's review:

The name expresses the very essence of an object and is inseparable from it. So too the name Jesus ...[40] The name, expressing the essence of an object, cannot be removed from it; with the removal of the name the object loses its meaning. One can see this also in simple things, for instance a glass ...[41] Call it by another name, it will no longer be a glass. Do you see how the name lies in the very essence of an object and merges into one with it, and to separate it is impossible without changing the understanding of the object? This comparison can be applied also to the name Jesus. (49)

The terminology here is similar to that of Eunomius but Ilarion does not use "essence" in the technical sense meant by St. Gregory; his point is rather that our understanding of things is inextricably tied to their names. Moreover, elsewhere in *Na Gorakh Kavkaza* he does use "essence" in the more technical sense and there acknowledges it to be "unconfessible" or unnameable, as does Fr. Antonii on numerous occasions. No other evidence could be found to link any imiaslavtsy to this aspect of Eunomius' teaching.

Eunomius also held that God's names in the very form in which we know them originated from him and were revealed directly by him. Against this St. Gregory said that they are rather human creations; they can be ultimately attributed to God as can everything, but they are directly attributable to man's will and freedom, to the rational faculty given by God to man. Therefore

---

[40] Here Troitsky jumps 400 pages from the introduction to the end of the book and a somewhat different context. This sentence actually reads not "So too the name ..." but rather "Thus the name 'Jesus' means Savior" (*Tak imia*, not *Tak i imia*), and the section goes on to talk about the name "Jesus."

[41] Ilarion's ellipsis.

to attribute them directly to God himself in Eunomius' sense is gross anthropomorphism. Cases where scripture says "God said" are not to be taken literally but are similar to passages which speak of the heavens proclaiming God's glory. In the same way, God does not speak to his prophets in human words but by a direct action on the soul, in response to which they use human words to express the meaning conveyed to them. Therefore God's names, even when scripture indicates that he personally spoke them, are strictly speaking not divine actions but human ones, the results of divine actions. From this Troitskii concluded that if the names are not divine actions then they do not even merit the title "divinity," much less "God himself." However, the imiaslavtsy had long before been accused of divinizing human letters and sounds and had frequently and explicitly denied it; it was not specifically in that sense of the word "name" that they called it God.

Against Eunomius's belief that God speaks exactly as humans do, St. Gregory argued that he has no need to do so. Words are symbols, necessary for rational thought and communication only for our bodily existence as humans; spiritual beings like God and angels have no need of them since for them their very thought is their word. And names, St. Gregory concluded, are merely a form of human words, disappearing with the sounds and having no independent existence. One must understand that the object named is one thing and the name itself another. Troitskii then drew from this some conclusions of his own: "All names are only symbols of things, signs, labels – [they are] placed on things by human reasoning *and by themselves are not at all connected with things*." (4) Because that connection exists only in the human mind, all names are separable from their objects; i.e. objects need not have names at all or their names can be changed, depending only on human will. The divine names are not fundamentally different:

> The names of God all by themselves (God's names in prayer will be discussed later) are inseparable from God only insofar as is all that exists; but any other relationship of them to God exists not in reality but only in our thought, which establishes a connection between the sign and the designated object. (54)

God's names are just "empty sound" like all others when considered "by themselves." They are not God's essence, they do not express his essence, they are not his actions and they do not even express his actions – "they are only signs, created by people, which **point to** either his characteristics or his actions in relation to the world and to man." (42) And in that function God's names actually do a poorer job than all others:

> [They] stand apart from their Prototype much farther than the names of other things from the things themselves, since on the one hand our conceptions about God correspond not to his essence but to his actions, and that only in part; and on the other hand all of our words are formed on the foundation of sensory conceptions and for expressing conceptions about God are unsuitable. (44)

To illustrate what Troitskii means: one of the divine names is "Holy Spirit," but in fact "spirit" as a word originally meaning simply "wind" or "breath" actually refers directly only to those material realities; it is applied to the third person of the Holy Trinity metaphorically and so is a poorer expression of him than it is of wind or of breath itself.

While ascribing this view to several early church fathers, Troitskii refers to the contemporary German linguist Max Muller as evidence that science confirms it:

Defending the connection of word and thought, and affirming the primeval religiosity of mankind, Max Muller also expresses the thought that divinity received nomenclature relatively late and that people could have been deeply religious without having any names for designating God. (58)

All was fine when these prehistoric people started applying names to their "sense of divinity," but they tended to understand names as "doubles" of objects with a reality all their own having "mystical connections" to the objects. That is precisely the origin of polytheism and idolatry, for while using many names to describe the one "divine sense" they began to ascribe divinity to those names themselves. Troitskii quotes Muller: "But ***names have a tendency to be made into objects, nomina are turned into numina (names into divinities), ideas into idols.***" (59; Troitskii's emphasis)

This then is precisely the error of the imiabozhniki. By honoring the name *per se* outside of its connection with God himself and speaking of it as a "spiritual essence" they have created an idol and/or have even introduced a fourth divine hypostasis into the Holy Trinity.

This accusation of Troitskii's is, however, merely a repetition of the same misrepresentation first made by Khrisanf and later by Abp. Antonii. None of the imiaslavtsy ever spoke about combinations of letters entirely out of context; in fact, "the name of God" ***by definition*** consists of those combinations in the context of their link in meaning to God himself.

In any case, the imiaslavtsy consistently explained that they were speaking of "God's name" in the wider sense meaning all of a person's thought about or knowledge of God. This position of theirs Troitskii acknowledges but asserts that it is merely obfuscation, for he believes "name" means specifically and exclusively the combinations of sounds. If the imiabozhniki mean by it "idea" or "thought" then they should simply say that. Be that as it may, they are wrong there too, he says. To equate our thought of God with God himself is even worse than doing that with his name, for thought exists only within the person. As St. Gregory of Nyssa said that "the name or *idea* are for Eunomius an idol which replaces God" (71), the same can be said of Eunomius's modern followers. Here Troitskii has at least not misrepresented his opponents' position, and it is precisely here that the fundamental difference between the two sides in the controversy is located. Before investigating that further, however, it will be helpful to review the practical consequences of his viewpoint.

Troitskii explains that God's names are indeed worthy of honor as religious symbols, in which respect they are identical in nature to all the others (the cross, icons, etc). Just as an icon consists of wood and paint, a name consists of paper and ink or vibrations in the air. Both serve merely to point to their prototype. This understanding is reflected in scriptural and patristic texts speaking of the cross and of icons in the same exalted terms used for God's name, and in statements like one made at the Sixth and Seventh Ecumenical Councils calling the words of the Gospel books an icon (image) of Christ. Therefore:

> The name of God is also a symbolic representation of God, is an *eikon*, just like a painted icon, and about icons, i.e. all representations of God, not excluding from that God's names, the fathers of the Church and the Seventh Ecumenical Council itself clearly and decisively teach that they are not God. (104)

In fact neither the fathers of the councils nor the councils themselves said that; the statement "icons are not gods" repudiates an understanding rather different from that held by the imiaslavtsy.

Fr. Antonii's approach to this issue is diametrically opposed to Troitskii's: whereas the latter calls names forms of "icons" in order to forestall ascribing too much significance to them, Fr. Antonii calls icons forms of "name" in order to link them to the wider meaning of "name" and thereby ultimately to ascribe greater significance to them. The difference may seem strictly semantic, but it involves radically different views of reality insofar as Troitskii's approach reflects his view that the link between symbol and object is entirely subjective and therefore not real. Fr. Antonii's approach on the other hand stresses the reality of that "link," subjective though it may be.

Another consequence of Troitskii's view is that since a name is just another symbol it cannot sanctify any of the others; icons, for example, are sanctified by the image itself painted on them, not by the name. The imiaslavtsy, of course, would reply that the image is itself the name, but Troitskii adds that in any case it is really only God himself who sanctifies:

> And so not one holy object is sanctified by the name of God, but all holy objects are sanctified by God's grace and only with invocation of the name of God or with the use of other holy symbols expressing the faith of the Church in God. (128)

Troitskii also repeats the accusations that imiabozhniki hold a magical and superstitious view of the effectiveness of God's name in prayer. Equating them with the medieval Jewish rabbis who, he explains, believed that pronunciation of the divine name always produced desired results, he lists a series of examples like the following:

> When the Philistine threw David high up, Avisaga pronounced "the name" and David remained hanging between heaven and earth, and later, with the help of the same means, came down. In general, in rabbinic literature "the name" often plays the role of a flying machine. (109)

The same superstitious view could be found in Christian apocryphal literature, where the name "Jesus" merely replaces the tetragrammaton. Examples:

> The name "Jesus" banishes fever, heals all diseases, raises a person into the air and lets him down again, helps a camel go through the eye of a needle, raises the dead, and drives out demons. (110)

The error in all this is that it places God in dependence on the whims of people and uses his name as something separate from him himself. Against such usage Troitskii explains that confession of God's name has no meaning except as an expression of faith, and points out that pronouncing God's name often does not result in miracles, and many miracles occur entirely without such pronunciation. From this he concludes that there is no "internal connection" between miracles and God's name. In general miracles occur for the purpose of strengthening and spreading the Christian faith, which is why God deigns to do some through otherwise unworthy people, rather than because of the power of the name itself. In any case only God himself through his grace actually performs miracles, not icons themselves, not names themselves, and not any of the other means used by humans to help bring them about. In this respect all holy symbols are nothing more than a means for grace.

This issue is directly tied to the sacraments, and here also Troitskii argues that only God himself and not his name is the effective or sanctifying force. In addition, since at the Seventh Ecumenical Council statements were made specifying that the eucharist is not an image (*eikon*) of the Lord's body and blood but rather truly is his body and blood, and since names are forms of icons, Troitskii concluded that God's name can neither be called a sacrament nor be equated to one:

> ... if the name of God by itself, as only a holy symbol **created by man**, cannot even compare with a sacrament in which **by God's will** the grace of God is inseparably united with a symbol, then it is clear that in no way can God's name sanctify the sacraments. (136)

And because the bread and wine are changed into the body and blood of the Lord solely by the action of the Holy Spirit, sacraments cannot even be equated with prayer:

> In this way the sacrament is effected by God and only by him; and in this the sacrament differs from prayer, where there are two actions, and the divine action is united with the human action. (138)

He specifies that sacraments are always effective, but, probably being conscious of thereby claiming for them essentially what the imiaslavtsy claim for God's name in prayer – and for which he accuses them of magic – Troitskii carefully explains that such could not be said of the sacraments:

> ... God performs the sacrament exclusively according to his good will, and not by any necessity; he performs it because he himself freely chose to unite for the whole time of the existence of the Church militant the actions of his grace which creates the new man with certain conditions, carried out by man. (138)

The pronunciation of God's name is but one of many conditions needed to effect the sacraments, others of which are material in nature, such as water for baptism. Therefore the imiabozhniki are guilty of a Lutheran view of the sacramental nature of the word, the unthinkable consequences of which would be that anyone, even non-Orthodox, could perform sacraments; the church hierarchy would not be needed; and even the sacraments themselves could be done away with.

Troitskii differentiates prayer from sacraments also in that pronunciation of God's name is not even one of the necessary conditions for the former as it is for the latter; as Theofan Zatvornik and others say, it can consist merely of a "striving of mind and heart" for God. The fact that names are unnecessary can even be seen in ordinary human interaction, where two people can communicate without knowing each other's names. Granted, Bulatovich calls the whole of a person's knowledge about God God's name, and the person's understanding of himself causing him to speak to God he calls the person's own name, but in doing so:

> Bulatovich simply named all the elements of prayer with the word "name," although no one has ever called these elements that until now; and thanks to such a method of proof he easily attained the needed result. Such a hussar-like audacious method of proof somewhat recalls the tale of the Catholic monk who called birds given to him during Lent by the names of various fishes, and so considered that he hadn't broken the fast. (123)

A truer analogy would be to say that Troitskii's position is like that of a person who gave the monk fishes but called them birds in order to accuse the monk of breaking the fast. Fr. Antonii had clearly shown that his understanding of "name" was solidly based on scriptural usage.

In addition to warning against exaggerating the importance of God's names in general, Troitskii also expends much effort to show that the name "Jesus" is not more important than the others. If it appears so in the book of Acts, that is simply because it was necessary for the spread of the new faith at that time. As for Philippians 2:9, St. Gregory of Nyssa interprets it not as exalting any one particular name above the others but rather as speaking of God's essential unnameability; "the name of Jesus" means "this special name which Jesus has," i.e., that of the unnameable God. And many patristic texts speak of "Jesus" as a human name. Khrisanf's applying it to the Lord's human nature is not nestorianism but rather rejecting such usage amounts to monophysitism.[42] This last charge is typical of Troitskii's apparently willful misunderstanding or misrepresentation of his opponents' position. Fr. Antonii had very clearly objected not simply to referring the name Jesus to the Lord's human nature but rather to doing so exclusively – and in that he was correct because the Lord's name designates his *person*, which is considered to be at once human and divine.

Troitskii goes on to refute the most important of the proof texts quoted by the heretics. He argues that some, i.e. those not of the canonical books of scripture or of canonized saints, are not authoritative anyway and may be dismissed. Statements of someone like John of Kronstadt cannot be used to help establish the teaching of the Church or at least cannot be placed on the same level as truly authoritative texts.

---

[42]Ascribing to Jesus Christ just one nature (*mono-physis*) was condemned at the council of Chalcedon in 453 as constituting a denial of his humanity, i.e., as confessing Christ as being truly God but not truly man.

Having thus immediately disqualified a large chunk of his opponents' witnesses, Troitskii deals with most of the rest by ascribing them to poetic or metaphorical language. Specifically, he claims that the imiabozhniki are guilty of confusing homonyms, i.e. words which are spelled and sound alike but which have completely different meanings. He provides an example of the nonsense that can arise from such confusion: the word "lock" can mean a lock of hair or the lock on a door, but just because of the words' similarity one does not speak of combing the lock of a door or of unlocking a lock of hair.[43]

The danger of confusing things in this way is especially present in theology since, as Max Muller confirms, all religious terminology consists of homonyms. "Name" is no exception. Not only can it mean a combination of letters, it can also mean glory and renown, and it can even be used simply as a synonym for the person itself. These meanings must not be confused. The latter usage is typical of Hebrew and can be seen especially in poetical texts like the Psalms. These often make use of parallelism wherein two clauses mean essentially the same thing; so texts like "Praise the Lord, sing praises to his name" prove nothing except that "name" is used there in a sense different from that of a symbol of sound. And there are many such uses of "name" which are simply peculiarities of the Hebrew language. Where texts say "the name of God" does a miracle, this means actually "God through his name." Likewise, in Hebrew "*bᵉshem*" (in the name) is used simply as a preposition meaning exactly the same thing as "*b*" (in), so that texts speaking of "faith in God's name" actually mean "faith in God himself."

---

[43]The example in Russian is *kosa*, which can mean 1) plaid or braid of hair; 2) scythe; 3) spit (small peninsula).

The same principle applies to texts like Isaiah 30:27: perhaps it really is a prophecy of the coming of Christ; but if so, then that is simply a different meaning of "name." Therefore all of the proofs offered by the imiabozhniki are convincing only for people who don't realize this peculiarity of language in general and Hebrew in particular.

The validity of this line of thinking is dependent on whether or not the various meanings of "name" are truly as unconnected and unrelated as Troitskii claims. And that is directly linked to the question of whether the symbols used to express those meanings are "in reality" unconnected with them. In a word, what Troitskii and all those opposing the imiaslavtsy were advocating is nominalism. And that is inevitably based upon objectivism. Both are foreign to Christianity.

Prof. Troitskii believes it is possible to conceive of an object "in itself" outside of all relation to any subject, entirely out of any and all context. But in fact an object inevitably presumes a subject; an object removed from all context is literally inconceivable, for the very act of conceiving places it in the context of the conceiver's mind. To speak of things "in or by themselves" insofar as that means "entirely out of context" is to speak untruth and unreality. Reality by its very nature includes **both** subject and object, and to divorce either from the other is fundamentally impossible. Reality is always as it were "dependent on" or "conditioned by" or "determined by" both subject and object, and to deny the proper role of each is to speak falsehood. This is why the belief that something can be isolated as "entirely subjective" and therefore "not real" is fundamentally false.

Nearly every page of Christian scripture abounds with evidence that it does not endorse such a view, but a few examples will suffice here. One is the story of Jesus watching all the rich people put great sums of money into the temple treasury and then seeing one poor widow throw in two cents and remarking: "Truly I say to you, this poor widow has put in more than all of them: for they all put in the offering out of their plenty, but she from her lack put in all the life that she had." (Lk 21:3-4) He did not say she put in more "relative to the others" but simply "truly ... she put in more." The objectivist has no choice but to deny the Lord's words and assert that no, she *really* did *not* give more.

Even the scriptural language itself argues against an objectivist view, as can be seen in the following saying of Jesus in Matthew:

> Either make the tree good and its fruit good; or make the tree bad and its fruit bad; for the tree is known by its fruit. (Mt 12:33)

In general Hebrew words meaning "cause to be" or "make to be" also mean "consider to be" or "judge to be." The talk here is not about doing things to trees but about rendering judgments, about naming. Yet it is expressed in terms of changing reality ("making to be"). The objectivist must argue that the two meanings are separate and incompatible – but this is an incompatibility felt neither by the Hebrew language nor by the author of Matthew's Gospel.

One of the very best examples of how Christianity balances the two "sides" or "aspects" of truth comes from Paul:

> ... we know that there is no idol in the world and that there is no god but one; for even if there are so-called gods whether in heaven or on earth, as indeed there are many gods and many lords, yet for

us there is one God, the Father, from whom are all things and we for him, and one Lord Jesus Christ, through whom are all things and we through him. (1 Cor 8:4-6)

The objectivist must reject "indeed there are many gods and lords" while the subjectivist must reject "there is no god but one," but Paul does not find it necessary to reject either. Indeed, a Christian cannot absolutely reject the truth of either without ultimately denying the whole of the Christian faith.

It is this "balance" of two seemingly conflicting truths that the opponents of the imiaslavtsy abandoned. In doing so they were constantly forced to interpret scripture as *"really meaning"* something quite different from its plain wording; so "the name above all names" "really means" no name at all; "God's name healed this man" *really means* God healed this man through his name; "faith in God's name" *really means* faith in God himself, and so forth. Such interpretations are not without validity – but to deny the equal validity of the sense of the plain wording is not merely to reject "literalism" but to project upon the texts a view of reality fundamentally different from the one they themselves reflect.

The point is that one cannot deny the reality or truth of "that which is subjective" without ultimately denying all reality, for all reality is experienced, is known subjectively. If, for example, I see a blue sky and another person sees it green, and I say that the other is wrong, I am essentially saying that his perception or his understanding or his knowledge of the sky is not the same as mine. He will say the same about mine. Which of us is correct? Which of us speaks "objective" truth? The only way to answer that is to assume that both of us are of one nature which would "normally" cause our perceptions of the same object to be the same, that our common nature also permits those perceptions to differ, and that we can determine what the "normal" perception should be for the object in question. The *only* basis for deciding that one of our understandings is "objectively true" and the other "objectively false" is thus to somehow decide that human beings *should* normally see there the color blue. In a simple case like the color of the sky we assume that human beings "should" see blue because most do, but in other areas deciding what "should be" is not so easy.

This is directly applicable to Christianity. The Christian believes that human persons can indeed know God because that capability is inherent in their common human nature insofar as all are made in his image and likeness. On that basis and only on that basis can Christians assert that the Christian understanding of God is "objectively" true and understandings contrary to it false. However, the Christian understanding or experience of God is ultimately just as "subjective" as all other understandings of God. And so there is even for Christians a sense in which all such understandings *are indeed* true and real. If we deny another reality because it is "only subjective" and because that which is subjective is *per se* "not real" – then we inevitably deny the truth and reality of our own understanding of God as well since it is equally subjective. There is thus in Christianity a paradox according to which the Christian must acknowledge that one and the same thought can be "true and real" and simultaneously "untrue and unreal." To completely repudiate either or to overemphasize either at the expense of the other is to distort reality itself. This is why Paul did not feel it necessary to deny unconditionally the reality of other gods; he in fact *could not* do so.

That is precisely where Troitskii erred, and it can be seen most concisely in the statement quoted above where he concludes that the connection between symbol and object is unreal because it "exists not in reality but only in our thought ..." Thought, memory, sensation, experience, perception, knowledge – all these do refer primarily to that which is "subjective," but this by its very nature cannot be divided or separated from that which is "objective." So even if it were true that the "connection" between symbol and object exists "only in thought" – it nevertheless truly, in reality, does exist.

But in fact that connection cannot exist "only in our thought" any more than the light by which we see exists "only in our thought." Just as we see because light through the organs of our eyes creates impressions on our mind, the "connection" between symbol and object can only be the result of some particular action. It must be created there by a very real action either of the person using the symbol or by other persons. Or by God. If in some literal or metaphoric sense God did give the name "Jesus" to his Son by sending his archangel Gabriel to the Virgin Mary – then the "connection" between that particular symbol and its referent is not happenstance. To deny the reality of that connection is to deny the reality of divine inspiration and to step outside of normative Christian belief. Moreover, Christianity acknowledges that divine inspiration is at work not only in isolated miraculous events but throughout the life of the Church – in the whole of scripture, in the writings of the saints, in the Church's prayers and worship services, etc. And so the same can be said of other symbols' relationship to reality that can be said of the name of Jesus.[44]

---

[44]This does not mean that all are of equal importance, of course.

In this context one can also see that Troitskii misinterpreted St. Gregory's statement that for Eunomius the "name or idea" of God had become an idol: by this St. Gregory meant not that *any* name or idea is by nature an idol, but rather that **Eunomius's** name or idea of God was such. This was so specifically because his "idea" of God was false; or in other words because it was incompatible with the one St. Gregory took to be normative – true – for Christians. St. Gregory would not have called his own "idea" of God an idol because he believed it to be true. At the same time, vital to the "true-ness" of his own "idea of God" was the conception that it was not absolutely all-encompassing, could not be identified absolutely with God. The idea that his understanding of God was in some sense inadequate was included in the very understanding itself, and that is why it did not become an idol for him. All of which is precisely the way the imiaslavtsy understood God's name.

As they pointed out, scripture does use "name" in the wider sense meaning all of our knowledge of God, and in that sense the name of God truly is God, God as we know him. And so they were also correct in saying that one cannot conceive of God apart from his name, for that is the same as saying that an object (God) cannot be conceived of without presuming a subject (his name, understood as our human understanding of him). It is the same as saying one cannot conceive of or know the "essence" of God. And so the faith of the imiaslavtsy – their understanding of God, their "name of God" – was precisely that of the Old Testament, of the New Testament, of St. Gregory of Nyssa, of St. Gregory of Palamas and of the entire Orthodox Christian tradition. With which their opponents' understanding was incompatible.

The importance of the difference between them and their opponents is by no means trivial. If a given person's understanding of God is contrary to the Christian view, a Christian must nevertheless admit that that person's God is indeed true and real for that person, though it is not the Christian God. The same is true for Christians: a person's understanding of God is God for that person. In that case, **all** that affects our understanding of God is of the utmost importance because it determines the personality of the God we serve. The essence of Christian life is to love and serve God – but we can only truly serve the God whom we know, and so to the extent that our knowledge of God is false, even though we call ourselves Christian we are in effect serving a false God. For Christians this knowledge of God, also called experience of God or communion with God, comes about in every aspect of life in the Church, yet some specific actions have a more direct or influential bearing on it than others. Among these would be the reading of scripture, prayer, participation in church services and sacraments, and so forth.[45] Therefore the words used in those contexts are of tremendous importance insofar as they constitute one of the most directly and obviously influential factors forming our understanding of God.

This is why so many prayers of the church consist almost entirely of names (i.e., descriptions of what God is like and what he has done). The Anaphora of St. Basil's Liturgy is typical:

> ... O Father of our Lord Jesus Christ, the great God and Savior, our Hope, who is the Image of your goodness, the Seal of your very likeness, showing forth in himself you, O Father – the living Word, the true God, the eternal Wisdom, the Life, the Sanctifica-

---

[45]Once again, they are not necessarily all of equal importance.

tion, the Power, the true Light, through whom the Holy Spirit was revealed ...

These prayers help ensure that all who are gathered together for common prayer are indeed speaking to the same God; through them we are not only speaking to God but forming our own understanding of him into the one common Christian understanding of him.[46]

Hence the specific words used to form that understanding – the names – are of the utmost importance. Troitskii's talk about homonyms is misleading; there is a significant difference between multiple meanings of one word, and multiple words which are spelled the same. The various meanings of one word are truly and intimately connected with each other and each reveals something about the other.[47] So when we speak of Jesus Christ as "Life" we are not *merely* using a different meaning for this word. We are indeed doing that, but at the same time the more general meaning of "life" shapes our understanding of Jesus Christ, and he in turn shapes our understanding of "life" itself. In this way the two become intimately tied together in our thought – and therefore in reality.

---

[46]Hence also the warnings about the Jesus Prayer – its short and concentrated form is at once its advantage and its danger. The person who does not already know Jesus well through years of having the scriptural image of Christ inculcated into him could easily pour into the name "Lord Jesus Christ Son of God" his own false meaning, and thereby be praying not to the Jesus Christ of Orthodox Christianity but to someone or something quite different.

[47]Of course, even the different meanings of homonyms are connected insofar as they share the same symbol expressing them. But this connection is far less significant.

It is for this reason that the names we use to refer to God are not to be treated lightly; we are not free to change them at will. This is why Orthodox Christians are so unwilling to change traditional symbols used to refer to God. This is why Orthodox Christians are reluctant, for example, to refer to God as "she"; we may not be able to specify precisely how the masculine pronoun "he" shapes our understanding of God, but in some way it inevitably does, and to change it would involve a change in our very understanding of him – and then we would actually be serving a different God.[48] It is in this context that Ilarion's statement about the name "Jesus" is to be understood: if we tried to call Jesus by a different name our understanding of him would indeed change – for us he himself would change and we would be worshiping a different Lord, a different God – because this name also bears other meanings which shape our understanding of the Lord.[49]

What this also means is that a difference in word usage always involves a different view of reality, for no word is a mere combination of letters out of all context. Ultimately there is no

---

[48] The same can be said of other symbols. In his role as celebrant of the Eucharist the priest serves as a symbol of Christ himself, and after thousands of years during which the Church has felt that being male was somehow significant in this context, to change that belief now could change the very understanding of God himself. Of course, the meanings of symbols are shaped by the culture in which they are used, and it is possible to argue that in our modern culture, abandoning this requirement would be the best way to maintain essentially the same understanding of God. In either case, the point is that the choice of symbol has serious ramifications for the faith, and neither blind conservatism nor thoughtless changes are appropriate.

[49] Including its etymological meaning "Savior" or "Victor" as well as the Old Testament persons who also bore it.

such thing as a difference "only in semantics." Each and every word has particular associations which influence and form the others. In some cases such influences are relatively insignificant but in others they are tremendously significant. For a Christian who takes his or her faith seriously, those referring to God belong in the latter group. And so the contention that God's names are really not all that important, that they can be changed at will, and that they serve only as a means for calling upon him are all fundamentally false. And the assertion that the word "God" can only mean God's "essence" is by no means a trivial error but is rather of the utmost seriousness.

Indeed, the consequences of the nominalist view for all of Christian life are enormous. Veneration of icons becomes meaningless, for then when we kiss an icon of Christ to venerate him, we are not "in reality" venerating Jesus Christ himself but only wood and paint. Even if Christ himself were to appear now in bodily form as he walked the earth in the first century we could never really venerate him himself – the apostles never did so, they never saw him himself, they never heard him himself, etc. – for his human body is not the "essence" of his divine person.[50] Ultimately every single action of Christian worship, every expression of worship and reverence – all of life – is made meaningless and worthless by the nominalist viewpoint. Nothing is true, nothing is real.

The point in all of this is not that the phrase "the name of God is God himself" cannot be interpreted in a way contrary to normative Orthodox Christian faith. One can do that with any

---

[50]Of course, the same can be said even of mere human beings. Who can define or locate the "essence" of a human person? Nominalism leads to a denial of reality on every level; one need not be a Christian to reject it.

given expression, as did Sabellius with as venerable a term as "Holy Trinity."[51] But this expression is indeed capable of a true interpretation, and that true interpretation was the one held by the imiaslavtsy. What's more, it cannot be rejected out of hand without ultimately denying the faith *in toto*. Proving it to be absolutely and unconditionally false requires disproving also scripture, church fathers, liturgy – ultimately the whole of the Christian tradition. Yet the condition for the exiled imiaslavtsy to be readmitted to communion with the church was precisely to sign a paper acknowledging that they "in no way" (*otniud*) considered the name of God to be God himself.

From an Orthodox Christian standpoint was the position of those who opposed the imiaslavtsy then heretical? If "heretical" were synonymous with "false" the answer would unquestionably be yes. The imiaslavtsy were certainly as justified in calling their opponents "imiabortsy" (name-fighters) for denying the divinity of God's name as the early church was in using the etymologically similar word "pneumatomakhoi" (spirit-fighters) to designate those who denied the divinity of the Holy Spirit. But the word "heresy" also tends to imply that a given position is stubbornly held even after it has been explicitly condemned by church authorities. That is not the case here. As *Moskovskiia Vedomosti* said of Nikon's use of military force, "This is much worse." Much worse. Here it is the church authorities themselves who not only proclaimed falsehood as truth, but also demanded signatures from their flock by which they would repudiate truth and embrace falsehood.

---

[51] Sabellius's view was termed "modalism," for he taught that God does not consist of three real persons but rather one only, who manifests himself in three different ways or "modes."

The Russian church was maneuvered into that position largely by political factors, and it would turn out to be largely political factors that would rescue it.

8
Truce

Debate Continues in Russia

Fr. Antonii Bulatovich's influential connections from before his tonsure turned out to be extremely useful. In March of 1913 Abp. Antonii had written to Fr. Jerome:

> It has been forbidden to allow Bulatovich into Petersburg ... he is lying low somewhere without a passport, as they say, around Petersburg among his acquaintances and is hiding himself. (Pakhomii 63)

In fact Fr. Antonii was carrying on his work of making personal appeals to the authorities in behalf of the imiaslavtsy and was writing letters, pamphlets, and books – right inside of St. Petersburg. A network of highly-placed friends from the litsey and from the regiment made possible a situation whereby the police did know where he was but did not inform the Holy Synod and did not hamper his activities in any way.[52] In late July the Synod tried again, deciding "to warn him that if he does not cut off his preaching about 'imiaslavie' the question will be raised about expelling Bulatovich out of the borders of Russia." (NV Aug 2:3) It was never able to make good on that promise.

Such warnings indicated that Fr. Antonii's efforts were not without effect. One, reported in nearly every major newspaper,

---

[52] Some of them: S. P. Beletsky, director of the police, Sergius Khripunov, general administrator of the lands of the crown, and prince Sergius Vasil'chikov. See Niviere 359-60.

was to make known a writing of Abp. Nikon from a decade back:

> The name of God is always holy; by it our saving sacraments are accomplished ... The name of God is the same as the inaccessible essence of God, revealing itself to people (qtd. in Vechevoi, 46).

The goal of course was not to embarrass Nikon but to reveal the true nature of the Synod's position – that what used to be orthodox had suddenly become heretical.

A more immediate reason for the expulsion warning came from Abp. Nazary of Odessa, who in July presented to the Holy Synod a number of letters from Antonii to the exiled monks in Odessa encouraging them to stand firm and not lose heart. Assurances in them that several bishops shared the monks' views, including Bp. Theofan and Bp. Germogen ("formerly of Saratov"), sparked also an investigation of the latter. The former had already been investigated: early in June the Synod held a series of secret meetings on the subject of Bp. Theofan's relationship with the imiaslavtsy. He was queried. He answered that he "views the matter of Bulatovich negatively" but that the name of God must be understood "mystically." Dissatisfied, the Synod asked again. No second reply was forthcoming. (See *Rech'* June 7:3) Apparently something similar happened with Bp. Germogen, for although the decision to investigate him was made in July, by late August newspapers were still reporting a rift between him and the Synod. There were also rumors that Bp. Trifon, Vicar of Moscow, and Bp. Tikhon of Ural were on the side of the imiaslavtsy (See *Rech'* Aug 10:2); but no evidence exists either that these or any other bishops supported the Athonite monks openly, or that the church authorities took punitive measures against any bishops for that reason. Nevertheless, it is probable that the cause of the imiaslavtsy was furthered behind the scenes by some Russian bishops whose actions will ever remain unknown to historians.

Support from the church's theologians was similarly low-keyed. When Fr. Florensky's magnum opus *Stolp i Utverzhdenie Istiny* (The Pillar and Foundation of Truth) appeared in 1914 it contained but one brief remark seemingly favorable to the views of the imiaslavtsy. Interpreting Matthew 18:19 ("For where two or three are gathered in my name, there I am among them"), he explained why such assemblies are always effective:

> Because – *gar*[53] – the gathering of two or three in Christ's name, the coming together of people into the mystical spiritual atmosphere around Christ, the partaking of his power of grace – transforms them into a new spiritual essence, makes of the two a particle of the body of Christ, a living incarnation of the Church (– **The name of Christ is the mystical Church!** –), enchurches them. (421)[54]

Sergius Bulgakov's lone contribution at this time was a short article entitled "The sense of the teaching of St. Gregory of Nyssa about names." Judging by what he wrote before and after (see Chapter 9), it is safe to assume that this was meant as a

---

[53] *gar* is the Greek word translated "For" at the beginning of Matthew 18:19.
[54] Notes in this section of *Stolp* refer to a long list of materials published by imyaslavtsy but list only the Synod's epistle for the opposing side. (See 782-3) Although some modern historians have listed Prince Eugene Trubetskoy (1863-1920) as supporting the imyaslavtsy, the *Russkaia Mysl'* article they base this on is in fact only a review expressing approval of Florensky's book. The case of Sergius Askol'dov (1870-1945) is similar: his *Russkaia Mysl'* article is not about imyaslavtsy or their doctrine but is a review of *Grazhdane Neba* (Citizens of Heaven) by V. Sventsitsky, a book about the growing phenomenon, attributed largely to the influence of *Na Gorakh Kavkaza*, of people living as anchorites in the Caucasus.

refutation of Prof. Troitskii's main theme, but it appeared in a little-known journal and can hardly have been influential.

The press mostly lost interest after the events of July ceased being news, but it remained generally sympathetic, sensing that a great injustice had been perpetrated on the Athonite monks. A common attitude:

> Bulatovich proves that the real teaching of the Athonites is completely unlike what the Synod thinks and that the synodal decision is based on error ... No one argues that divinization of the very name "Jesus" sounds like fetishism. But why insert such content into the idea of the Athonite teaching? By its idea it simply means to say that the name "Jesus" is no simple name, that it is sanctified already by the very fact of assimilation of this name to the incarnated Son of God, that now one cannot treat it like other names. With such fundamental positions each Christian can agree. One can even let the Athonites in their mystical strivings go somewhat farther than ordinary veneration of the name "Jesus." What harm in that? (TsOV 1913 42:2)

Others found it convenient to support the monks for political reasons, as turned out to be the case in the State Duma.[55] When in February of 1914 with the aid of the Octobrist party the Athonite monks submitted to the Duma a formal complaint (*zapros*) charging that their rights had been infringed (see in Vechevoy 48-9), their cause was taken up by "center/left" factions and opposed by "right" factions. The latter, generally supportive of autocracy and church understood as one indivisible package, saw this *zapros* as an attack against the church itself (which it certainly was for many of the "lefts"), and was able to get it sent to committee. There it seems to have died without

---

[55] The Russian equivalent of a national legislature.

accomplishing anything significant. The left factions brought up the issue again in April as an example showing why the Synod's budget should be reduced, but there it was once again only a means to a political end. Ultimately it had little or no influence on the course of the controversy itself.

For a time the Synod's intransigence had actually been unavoidable, for, having yielded jurisdiction in the case to the patriarch of Constantinople by its August 27 decision, it was awaiting instructions from him. After a delay of three months Patr. Germanos replied with a letter dated December 11 which was received in St. Petersburg in mid-January. He said leniency would be inappropriate for the "stiff-nicked and unrepentant" monks. Measures prescribed by the canons for "unrepentant heretics" should be applied with all stringency (*epakribōs*) for "reliable and full stigmatization and punishment, and for protection of the faithful from the deception and destruction that comes from them." But since now they are outside of the borders of the Ecumenical Patriarchate, such measures should be decided on and undertaken by the Church of Russia, "within whose borders the heresy of the imiabozhniki (*onomatotheitōn*) both appeared from the beginning and exists now." Any who repent should be restored to their former status, with one exception:

> But since it is not improbable that even having shown repentance they will cause problems and scandals upon returning to the Holy Mountain, we have decided that none of them may return to the Holy Mountain, which we consider just and proper (*Epistolē Patriarkhikē*)

The Russian press reported that this letter produced an "extremely unpleasant impression" in "higher spiritual circles" since the patriarch not only declined to handle the unpleasant business of holding a court against the monks but also would not allow their return to Athos. Most saw it as more evidence that he was acting strictly from nationalistic motives, not wanting to allow Russians to gain a majority on Athos again. The Synod decided to have the Russian ambassador to Constantinople explain to Germanos the "inappropriateness of his point of view" as well as to send a complaint directly from the Synod itself.

It seems likely that their analysis of his motives was not groundless, but there were other reasons for the decision as well: after the exiles' departure the Athonite *Iera Koinotes* had decided on July 31/August 13 that none of them should be allowed back. And it was not only the Greeks who had expressed that view; the Russians who remained, under the leadership of Jerome and Misail, expressed similar wishes to the Holy Synod. The depth of feeling among them on the subject can be seen in a booklet entitled "The truth about the events that occurred at St. Panteleimon's monastery during the first half of 1913," published by the monastery and signed by "Abbot and brotherhood." Designed to counter the bad press in Russia concerning Nikon's work, it even resorted to outright lies, claiming, for example, that the only condition given the imiaslavtsy for being allowed to remain on Athos was to promise to live there peacefully. The prevailing attitude of those left in authority on Athos can also be seen in this pamphlet's account of the fate of one imyaslavets, Archimandrite Arseny, who had served as abbot of St. Andrew's after David and who had been too ill to depart with the rest. Three months later because he would not "repent" he was allowed to die without the sacraments and was not even given a Christian burial.

Whatever Germanos's reasons, the Synod could no longer claim the matter was out of its jurisdiction, so on February 5 Fr.

Antonii petitioned for a church court. The request was granted, but the *opredeleniye* (decision) of February 14-18 granting it spoke as if the court's decision were a foregone conclusion. The text of the *opredeleniye* begins by recounting not only the patriarchal and synodal condemnations of the false teaching but also the "crimes" committed by the monks on Athos and their continuing refusal to listen to "the voice of the Church." In conclusion it calls to court only twenty-five of them, those who had been "on Athos especially stubborn partisans of the false teaching and the most zealous spreaders of it, and in Russia did not display an inclination to repentance but continued to defend their delusion." These monks could avoid the inevitable only by repenting, for which they would be given ample opportunity:

> [Since] outside of the Church there is no salvation, and with excommunication from the holy Church the imiabozhniki will inevitably destroy their own souls, the Holy Synod, in motherly love for perishing Christian souls, has considered it necessary that the imiabozhniki be given admonishments even in court.

Monks known for their "strict monastic life" were to be chosen to admonish them even before the court's formal opening in hopes that even then they might repent. Each was to be admonished individually and each was to appear before the court individually, their cases considered completely separately. The Moscow synodal office would hold the court, but its decisions were to be approved by the Synod itself.[56]

Church court or kangaroo court? With each monk being called to appear singly before a panel of judges at meetings closed to

---

[56] For the judges' names see the *opredeleniye* (TsV 1914 9:62-3), TsV 1914 11:598, NV Apr. 3:2, and MV May 8:3-4, each with a slightly different list.

public and reporters, this would be no open debate as the imiaslavtsy had hoped for. And no attempt at mutual understanding; they would merely listen while their judges "admonished." Recognizing the hopelessness of the situation, on the eleventh of April twelve of them headed by Fr. Antonii sent an announcement to the Synod declaring that they would not appear at court and were breaking communion with the Russian Holy Synod. In doing so they nevertheless asserted that they remained as always loyal to the Orthodox Church:

> We the undersigned announce to the Holy Synod that we always unchangeably abode and now abide in the teaching of the Holy Orthodox Church and do not allow ourselves to depart one iota from the teaching of the Holy Orthodox Church ...

It was the Synod itself which departed from the Church's teaching, and many efforts were expended to convince it of its error:

> However the Holy Synod not only did not pay attention to our petitions but continued to abide in the same opinions and condemned our veneration of the divinity of the name of God – which is in agreement with patristic teaching – as a heresy. And it named us, orthodox monks, with the unjustified and offensive name "imiabozhniki."
>
> Concluding from this that the aforementioned incorrect teaching about the name of God is not a mistake which has crept in by chance but has been received by the Synod henceforth irreversibly as a dogma – we with regret and sorrow are forced, for the sake of preserving the purity of the Orthodox faith: TO RENOUNCE EVERY SPIRITUAL RELATION (*obshchenie*) WITH THE ALL-RUSSIAN SYNOD AND WITH ALL WHO AGREE WITH IT, UNTIL CORRECTION [BY IT] OF THE DESIGNATED ERRORS AND UNTIL ACKNOWL-

EDGEMENT [BY IT] OF THE DIVINITY OF THE NAME OF GOD, IN AGREEMENT WITH THE HOLY CATECHESIS AND THE HOLY FATHERS.

Therefore we also announce that we refuse to appear before the court of the Moscow Synodal Office. (Antonii, *Imiaslavie*, 166-9)

In time more than 300 Athonite monks signed this declaration. Nevertheless, as *Novoe Vremia* reported, it "didn't make a big impression" on the members of the Synod. "The fickle character of A. Bulatovich, in their opinion, allowed one to expect surprises." (Apr. 20:6)

The Athonite Monks Vindicated ... Sort Of

Soon something did make a very big impression on them indeed, something from above rather than from below. Already in the fall of 1913 rumors had been rampant that "higher circles" were very unhappy with the way the Athonite affair had been handled and that Abp. Antonii, Abp. Nikon, and Sabler were all going to lose their posts. It turned out that only Abp. Antonii was actually dropped from the Synod that fall, but the consensus was that the move was forced upon Sabler against his will. Indeed, the two were so close that the archbishop reportedly suffered no loss of influence in the Synod's affairs; Sabler even traveled to Zhitomir in order to confer with him regarding the next summer's agenda for the Synod. Then the following spring the Synod's bowing to requests for a church court was again ascribed to "higher circles." One may wonder, what "circles" were higher than the supreme church authority?

While ascribing much of this to Fr. Antonii's "connections," the press never named them. However, it did name one very important "connection" for the imiaslavtsy in general: the grand duchess Elizaveta Fedorovna (the tsar's sister-in-law), who had published *Na Gorakh Kavkaza* on her own means. And there is evidence that Rasputin too may have supported the imiaslavtsy, perhaps mainly out of personal dislike of Sabler (see Nivière, 364). Such connections could, and apparently did, reach the tsar himself, for on April 15 he addressed a note to Sabler:

> On this feast of feasts [Easter] ... my soul grieves for the Athonite monks, from whom has been taken away the joy of partaking of the holy mysteries and the comfort of being in church. Let us forget the quarrel ... the court should be canceled and all the monks ... placed in monasteries, their monastic rank returned, and they should be permitted to serve as priests (qtd. in Katsnelson, *Po neizvedannym*, 187; ellipses his)

The order itself was not publicized, but the results were swift and dramatic. Five days later the ober-prokuror presided at a meeting in Moscow where he "conveyed his instructions concerning the matter of the Athonite monks" to Metropolitan Makarius. And when both Makarius and Bp. Modest of Verey were called to Petersburg on the next day, *Moskovskiia Vedomosti* reported that "their departure is attributed to the new direction which the matter of the imiabozhniki must now take." (Apr. 22:3)

On the twenty-fourth at a special service held in Moscow the hierarchs of the court participated in a church service at which nine of the Athonite monks, who had expressed their "desire to be received into communion with the Orthodox Church," were officially received. Neither signatures nor repudiations were required of them. They only had to announce that they adhered to all the teachings of the Church, neither adding to nor subtracting from them, and to confirm that announcement by kissing the Gospel book and the cross. It was explained that the previously "distrustful" attitude of these nine toward the synodal court was based on a "misunderstanding," and Bp. Modest was sent to Petersburg to visit the others to determine if perhaps their attitude too was based on a misunderstanding.

And so a new petition, which Fr. Antonii had sent to the Synod on April 22 expressing willingness to negotiate directly with it instead of the Moscow court, turned out to be unnecessary. Upon returning Modest reported that his mission was successful:

> The Athonite monks made a good impression on me. They are humble, cherish the dogmas of the Orthodox Church [and] recognize the divinely established hierarchy. The particularity of their opinion about the name of Jesus is explained by their not being familiar with our commonly-received theological language, and they express their thoughts in such words which for us have a somewhat different shade [of meaning] ... Fr. Antonii Bulatovich, a former officer of the guard, gives the impression of a very intelligent person as well as of one well-read in the writings of the holy fathers. From a long discussion with him I got the impression that his soul suffers from the noise raised around his name, which he fears can engender the thought that he supposedly goes against the Orthodox Church. He is amazed, why do people not want to understand him. He doesn't consider his opinion about the name of God a dogma, doesn't foist it on others, but only desires that the coming council will pronounce on it and decide the theological argument which has arisen. (MV May 8:2)

The hierarchs, headed by Metr. Makarius, decided not to call the monks to court; to receive them back into the church; and to admit them into Modest's Znamensky monastery. Thenceforth in order to be received into communion with the Church, any of the Athonite monks would need only to announce to their local bishops that they "believe as the Orthodox Church believes" and to confirm their sincerity by kissing Gospel and cross. Their things taken from them at Odessa were to be sent to them at whatever monasteries they wound up in. The Moscow synodal office also promised to take into consideration their request to be given a skete of the monastery of Simon the Canaanite in the Caucasus (where Ilarion himself once dwelt), and to establish it with funds drawn from the Athonite monasteries from which they had been expelled. Though not explicit in the court's decision, future events showed that their request for consideration of the theological issues at the upcoming council was approved. Likewise their request that the name "imiabozhniki" be dispensed with was apparently received favorably, for Metr. Makarius called them "imiaslavtsy" in his notice to the Holy Synod of the court's decision. In that notice he explained that the decision was based on documents sent to the court and to the Synod by the imiaslavtsy:

> Upon examination of these "confessions" and "announcements" the synodal court found ... data for the conclusion that ... there are no bases for [their] departure (*otstupleniia*) from the Orthodox Church on account of their teaching about God's names. [Specifically this is evident in their statement that]: "I repeat, by calling the name of God and the name of Jesus – God and God himself, I am neither venerating God's name separately from God himself and as some kind of special Divinity, nor am I divinizing the very letters and sounds and chance thoughts about God" (qtd. in OIB 211).

Accordingly on May 18 Fr. Antonii and the others sent a new announcement to Metr. Makarius thanking him for absolving them of the charge of heresy; rescinding their notice of April 11; and asking that he inform the Synod of that fact. While reaffirming their faithfulness to all of the Church's dogmas, they did not back down from their beliefs concerning the name of God:

> ... we in agreement with the teaching of the holy fathers confessed and do confess the divinity and divine power of the name of the Lord. This teaching we do not raise to the level of a dogma, for it has not yet received conciliar formulation, but we expect that at the coming council it will be formulated and dogmatized. Therefore we, in agreement with the teaching of the holy fathers [and] in the words of the ever-memorable John of Kronstadt, both said and do say that the name of God is God himself, [and] the name of the Lord Jesus Christ is the Lord Jesus Christ himself. We understand this teaching not in the sense of divinization of a created name, but rather we understand it spiritually, in the sense of the inseparability of God's name from God while calling upon him, and in the sense of divinely-revealed truth, which is the action of divinity. (NV May 23:6)

They were still "deeply offended by the actions and words of archbishops Antonii and Nikon, especially the former, for he is the main culprit in the Athonite trouble." After briefly recounting the deeds of these two the monks added:

> May God reward them according to their deeds if they do not repent. As for those many slanders which Abp. Nikon raised against us in his report and in his booklets, as, for example, that the trouble arose supposedly because of separatist dissension, from a striving for robbery and power, because of reasons of a revolutionary character, etc. – may the Lord God forgive him this and we forgive him. May God also forgive him those tragedies which he caused us personally by his cruel-heartedness and injustice.

Finally they repeated their request for a skete in the Caucasus (which was, apparently, never granted).

"In that way, thanks to the tact and gentleness of Bp. Modest, the formerly stormy matter of the Athonite monks has been resolved peacefully and calmly" reported *Novoe Vremia* on May 8. A rather strange "resolution," however. It was never reported in any of the Synod's publications, although they had reported every condemnation against the imiaslavtsy and had thoroughly covered the start of the court's proceedings. Troitskii kept up his polemics against them. Abp. Antonii kept up his polemics against them.[57] As late as 1916 many were still being refused the sacraments, even on their deathbeds (see Nivière, 366). And when the matter was taken up at the 1917 council, the monks were still officially called "imiabozhniki."

In these developments and in what preceded them a definite pattern can be seen. Several times major decisions were forced on the Synod against its will from outside – but since in their implementation the Synod was left to its own devices, it did all it could to circumvent the intent. So when Abp. Antonii was dropped from the Synod, Sabler still went to confer with him on the following year's program. When the Synod found itself obliged to hold a church court it created one where the result was a foregone conclusion. And in its eyes this last situation would have been worst of all, for it was a humiliating reversal: suddenly the stubborn stiff-necked unrepentant blasphemous deluded heretics were really orthodox all along but had been misunderstood. All the public condemnations, all the work of "admonition" on Athos, all the cruelties of the expulsion, all the ensuing propaganda – all one big mistake. Small wonder the

---

[57]Even as late as 1916 he had his new diocese of Khar'kov publish a book entitled *Holy Orthodoxy and the imiabozhnik heresy.*

Synod had no desire to publicize the court's decision or even to carry it out in good faith. It didn't.

As one religious publication noted in October of 1913, prematurely foreseeing resolution of the Athonite affair, such behavior was lamentably typical of the contemporary Russian Church:

> Purely chance circumstances helped the Athonites attain a more favorable attitude toward their case. It is this that is sad. If Antonii Bulatovich had no connections, Antonii and Nikon would be sitting on the Synod and there would not even be talk about reconsideration. In such a way the church world turns out to be in dependence on external factors, and the establishment of truth is attained thanks to external interference. The thought involuntarily arises: just how normal is such a situation of church affairs? In the press it is justifiably pointed out that the Athonite history serves as a graphic demonstration of in what untrustworthy hands lies the guidance of the ship of Church. The tactics shown in the matter of the Athonites are common tactics of the contemporary ecclesiastical course. Not to consider public opinion, not to want to hear objections, to act according to personal views and sympathies – there is the program of contemporary leaders. Consequently they are applied everywhere, and only external circumstances occasionally restrain catastrophes like the Athonite affair (TsOV 1913 42:2).

Since the same course of action could be seen in a series of church reforms being pushed through by "the party of Antonii of Volynia," the author expresses hope that the departure of that party's leader might mean a change. "However, signs of such a change are for the time being not visible."

This state of affairs, while indeed sad, is not exactly an anomaly unknown to the history of the Orthodox Church. One need only think of the triumph of Orthodoxy over the iconoclasts, which was effected both times by imperial decree. Nevertheless, icon veneration would have been as short-lived as iconoclasm had it been rejected by the masses of church members and if its defense had not been taken up by brilliant theologians who convincingly showed the errors of their opponents. In the case of imiaborchestvo more work of this nature needed to be done. That task was undertaken again largely by one person – Hieromonk Antonii Bulatovich.

9
Name as Sacrament

A Sequel to Apologiia Very

Soon after Russia entered World War I in 1914 Fr. Antonii successfully petitioned to serve the front-line troops as a priest of the Red Cross, and so most of the war he spent at the front under conditions which precluded his continuing to write books and articles. Nevertheless he kept up his theological defense of the divinity of God's name during occasional breaks which he would spend with his sister in Petersburg. Some of those were necessitated by the recurrence of a lifelong eye ailment that made it nearly impossible for him to bear any light at all, so he would do his typing in a darkened room.[58] His sister Mary Orbeliani remembers that "the whole night was this tap-tap-tap-tap, the whole night. And the room was next to my son's room ... He wrote, wrote, wrote, wrote, wrote, wrote ... hours and hours and hours" (Tape 9). Her son, who apparently learned how to sleep to the clatter of a typewriter, recalls:

> When I knew Bulatovich, my uncle, during 1915-16 in Petersburg ... he was living with us in a dark room because of his eyes. He was typing endless letters and pamphlets about his

---

[58]Katsnelson says there are reports that he not only performed priestly functions but also was awarded a medal for valor in rescuing a wounded soldier under enemy fire and even for leading an attack. However his sister does not believe that could be true, because as a monk he would not have done so, because she would have heard about it, and because the very eye ailment that forced him occasionally to go on leave precluded military activities. See *Po neizvedannym*, 189 and Orbeliani Tape 8.

imiaborchestvo. He was typing blind in the darkness and typing well, with very few errors. (Letter dated Jan. 29, 1977)

From these numerous works one series of articles remains as important a theological monument as his original *Apologiia*, particularly as published in book form under the title *Opravdanie Very v Nepobedimoe, Nepostizhimoe, Bozhestvennoe Imia Gospoda Nashego Iisusa Khrista* (A Justification of Faith in the Invincible, Incomprehensible, Divine Name of Our Lord Jesus Christ). Remarkably, these articles found publication in one of the more influential independent religious publications of Russia – Vladimir Skvortsov's *Missionerskoe Obozrenie* (Missionary Review). Skvortsov, of all people! He whose publications had rivaled Abp. Antonii's for virulence in attacking the imiaslavtsy made an abrupt about face some time during 1915 and adopted their point of view. Specifically how this came about is not known, but it serves as yet another indication that when people began to listen to the imiaslavtsy themselves as well as to their opponents, it was the former who benefited. And with the forum offered by *Missionerskoe Obozrenie* many more had an opportunity to do that listening.

While the new work covers many of the same themes found in *Apologiia*, one can see a shift in emphasis. Where the earlier one focused on the name as divinely revealed truth, i.e. as knowledge of God, the new work focuses more on the name as act of naming, as confession of faith. Ironically, Fr. Antonii found extensive support for his position in St. Gregory of Nyssa – drawing primarily upon extracts quoted by Troitskii himself. St. Gregory sums up his own attitude toward God's names in one key passage where he describes the difference between himself and Eunomius, who had said that the "sacrament of piety" (*to tēs eusebeias mystērion*) consists in "accuracy of dogmas":

Name as Sacrament

> But we, having learned from the holy voice that "If one is not born again through water and spirit, he will not enter into the kingdom of God" and that "Whoever eats my flesh and drinks my blood, that person will live forever," are convinced that the sacrament of piety is established (*kyrousthai*) by the confession of the divine names, I mean of the Father and of the Son and of the Holy Spirit; and salvation is confirmed (*kratynesthai*) by communion of the mystical rites and symbols. (PG 45:880B)

While the imiabortsy constantly called the names of God nothing more than a means for calling on him and in the sacraments considered it to be merely one among many "conditions" which needed to be fulfilled, St. Gregory thus spoke of confessing God's names as the very foundation of Christian life. Fr. Antonii notes that in response to Eunomius's lumping names, symbols, and rites together to denigrate the importance of all of them, St. Gregory separated confession of names from use of rites and symbols, spoke first of the former, and used a stronger word to express its importance.

The key word here is "confession." The imiaslavtsy had never emphasized the saving effectiveness of simply "knowing" God's names as had Eunomius, nor had they stressed mere "pronunciation." They did assert that pronunciation of God's name was itself significant, but this was precisely because to some degree it implies a confession of faith, just as prayer in general implies faith insofar as one would not pray if one did not have some faith that someone is listening. And it is in this act of prayer/confession of faith that the very essence of Christian life – of salvation – consists. Saint Paul wrote: "If you confess with your mouth the Lord Jesus and believe in your heart that God raised him from the dead, you will be saved; for with the heart is believed unto righteousness, but with the mouth is confessed unto salvation" (Rom 10:9, 10).

The imiabortsy spoke about prayer to "God himself" and about confession of "God himself" outside of or without God's names, but this is in fact impossible physically and epistemologically. Insofar as one speaks of confession with the lips, human words are required. And insofar as one speaks of prayer of mind and heart, human thought is required. Fr. Antonii challenges: "... if the imiabortsy consider prayer 'in the name' of the Lord 'stupidity,' and find it possible to pray to God directly, passing by his name, then let them show us an object to call up in our mind during prayer that would not be his name ..." (200)

Confessing God's name is thus the ultimate "sacramental" act upon which all others depend. And here is a radical difference between imiaslavtsy and imiabortsy: the latter understood "the sacraments" to be a few special acts *by their very nature* different from prayer and the rest of Christian life, the *only* absolutely reliable sources of divine grace. Fr. Antonii, on the other hand, affirms that not only is naming the Lord *the* fundamental sacramental act, it is the very act by which the "sacraments" themselves are made effective. As he had done before in his *Apologiia*, he again here stresses that the foundation for the reliability of the sacraments' effectiveness is in fact to be found in the Lord's promises concerning his name. These include Old Testament promises such as "all who call upon the name of the Lord shall be saved" (Joel 2:32/3:5), but for Christians the promises made by the Lord Jesus Christ himself are most important: "Truly, truly I say to you, whatever you ask the Father in my name he will give you" (John 16:23; see also 14:13 and 15:16). This is the reason for the numerous commandments to have faith "in the name of Jesus Christ" (e.g. 1 John 3:23), to have life "in his name" (John 20:31), and to find salvation itself "in his name." (Acts 4:12, 2:21) And this is why St. Paul spoke of the divine name and the Holy Spirit as being equally the effective agents in baptism: "... but you were washed, you were sanctified, you were justified in the name of the Lord Jesus Christ and in the Spirit of our God." (1 Cor 6:11)[59]

If then we do not hesitate to say that baptism "is" the rebirth of which the Lord spoke, not merely a means toward that end; and participation in the Eucharist "is" communion with God, not merely a means toward that end; dare we speak in less exalted terms about the use of God's name in prayer and in confessions of faith? Indeed, is not one reason for speaking as we do of those "sacraments" the belief that they absolutely reliably accomplish the thing for which they are the means – so that means and end ultimately cannot be separated? The same must then be said of prayer, which consists essentially of pronouncing God's names – whether verbally or mentally.

As for the cries of "magic," Fr. Antonii observes that "Of course, the name of Jesus cannot save the one who, although calling upon the name of the Lord Jesus Christ, boldly transgresses God's commandments; just as communion of the body and blood does not justify the unrepentant sinner." (77) Nor does a belief in prayer's consistent effectiveness imply that this occurs without reference to God's will – rather, of his own good will he made certain promises, and his promises are absolutely and consistently reliable. Troitskii's error was in applying those promises only to a few particular rites from which he excluded prayer and confession of faith in God's name. Yet it

---

[59]Cf. the priest's words in the Orthodox rite of baptism and chrismation: "you are baptized. You are illumined. You have received anointment with the holy chrism. You are sanctified. You are washed in the name of the Father and of the Son and of the Holy Spirit. Amen."

is precisely to the latter that the promises are expressly made. That is why our faith is truly "in the name of the Lord Jesus Christ." And it is why the "faith of the Church" cited by the Synod's May 18 epistle as the basis for the sacraments is ultimately the name of God. One may draw a direct parallel to God's reason for acting in the Old Testament. Just as he saved the Israelites not for the sake of their own goodness and worthiness but "*for my holy name's sake*" (see Ezek 36:22-3) – so too now he saves Christians not because of their personal holiness but for his name's sake, specifically for the sake of his name Jesus – the Savior.

This certainly does not mean, however, that the individual's faith is irrelevant; what is objectively offered must be, and might not be, subjectively received. Neither factor is independent from the other, as is shown in Peter's words about the lame man who was miraculously healed: "And on account of faith in His name, His name strengthened this man whom you see and know, and the faith which is through it gave him this health ..." (Acts 3:16) Here the name is clearly not just a "means" but is God's very power or grace. "One wonders, what more indisputable witness about the divine power of the name of Jesus Christ need we search out in scripture?" questions Fr. Antonii. (88) Yet there is a balance in this text between "name" and "faith," and it is that balance which the imiabortsy have abandoned:

> But so that no one would think that this name is some kind of magical power, which by a mere combination of letters and by the power of mere pronunciation must work miracles, Peter added "and faith, which is for His sake, gave him complete healing." Our opponents ignore the power of the first half of the text and concentrate only on the second; seizing upon these words they say, "There, you see, not the name of the Lord healed the lame man, but faith in him himself." However, to the degree that it would be

Name as Sacrament

unorthodox to affirm that only the power of Peter's pronouncing the name of Jesus Christ without any co-action of his faith healed the lame man, to the same degree it would be unorthodox to affirm that it was not the power of the name of Jesus Christ that co-worked this miracle, and reject the words "His name strengthened him."

But our opponents object to us: "In the world there is only one power of God, what other power have you found in his name?" Of course, in the world there is only one power – of God; as also in man – only one power of his essence. However, as in man we distinguish the powers of his members, so also in the world we distinguish various gifts and powers of God which are all various energies of him; and insofar as it would be foolish to deny the right to say about a person that he did something by the power of his right hand or left, likewise it would be foolish to deny the right to say that some or other miracle was co-worked by the power of God's name. But it is in this that the difference between our understanding of the name of God and the understanding of our opponents consists: while we see in God's name as it were his living hand, our opponents want to see in it some kind of inanimate instrument, not consubstantial with him and having no power in itself. (88)

In its prayers the church constantly sings of the power of the cross – "O invincible, incomprehensible, divine power of the honorable and life-creating cross, do not forsake us sinners." (Compline) By the power of your cross preserve us, O Lord"; "By the power of your cross save us, O Lord." (Matins) Now in fact the cross's power is the power of the name insofar as it is a graphic depiction of the name of the crucified Jesus:

> But if the powers of both cross and name are identical, then are not the cross and the name identical by essence? By their external side the name of Jesus and the cross are identical symbols, as the

Catechesis says, ... repeating the words of St. Chrysostom "that the name pronounced *by the motion of the lips* is the same as the sign of the cross," symbolically depicted by the movement of the hand. And so, by its external side the name of the Lord Jesus is a symbol of sound, calling to mind the very same truth as does the symbol of the cross. But are both identical also by their internal side? Of course not, for how can the cross be identical with the name when the cross by its essence has no internal side in itself, but the name does have? The cross by its essence is either material, or writing in lines and colors, or writing in the air by the motion of the hand; but a name *by its essence is thought*, which can be expressed symbolically, but can be thought also without external sound-symbols. Therefore if about the power of the cross one can say it is God himself, nevertheless to say this about the cross itself is inadmissible, and therefore the saints, calling the name of Jesus "Light," "God," "Master"; calling religious-moral truths "God," calling the Jesus prayer "God," calling the gospel word "God" (see Sts. Simeon, Hesychios, Gregory, Makarius, Theofilakt, Justin) – nowhere permit themselves so to name the cross. (141-2)

And so the two understandings of "God's name" are essentially inseparable: by its "objective" side the name is truly divine power, "energy" in Palamite terminology; while by its "subjective" side it is our experience or knowledge or understanding of that divine power. To consider either apart from the other is literally impossible, and this is why scripture, the saints, and church services use the word "name" in both meanings interchangeably.

Dare we consider such word usage in scripture happenstance? Fr. Antonii objects to all attempts at attributing it merely to poetic turns of phrase or meaningless quirks of the Hebrew language: "... such an equating of church truth to worldly poetry, which for the sake of adornment permits every distortion and exaggeration, we consider completely inadmissible, for the hymns of our Church were written by Saints who for the sake of poetic adornment would absolutely not dare to trample upon dogmatic truth." (7)

The same could be said of scripture itself, and here Fr. Antonii could have developed the thought farther than he did. To say that one understands the Bible as speaking truthfully and realistically does not necessarily mean "literally" – but it does mean that the way it expresses the truth remains the best way. One can take "anthropomorphic" expressions like those referring to the eyes and ears of the Lord as an example: these are not to be understood in exactly the same sense as when applied to humans – yet they serve to express important truths about God, and the Christian is bound to reject as untrue any statement that God "in no way/absolutely does not" have eyes and ears. We can attempt to describe what such phrases mean, but the scriptural phrases themselves remain the last word and final authority. The same is true of the eucharist. Over the centuries there have been countless attempts at explaining what the words "This is my body, this is my blood" mean – and such attempts are not without value – but ultimately one can only understand the eucharist by experiencing it, i.e., by partaking of the sacrament.

The very word "sacrament" means "mystery" – that which we do not fully comprehend – and it applies equally well to the very words of scripture. And so the very fact that scripture does use "God's name" as a synonym for "God" indicates that in some sense God's name truly is God himself. If we do not understand how this can be, or cannot explain how, then this is not necessary. The only way to understand is the way of experience – the way of calling upon God's name in prayer.

On the other hand, Fr. Antonii asks: if in Hebrew "in the name of" really is perfectly synonymous with "in," and that usage means absolutely nothing in itself, then why not translate it accordingly, everywhere replacing "in the name of the Lord" with "in the Lord" and so forth? As they are now, all such expressions in scripture and church prayers would have to be considered as mistranslations, all together constituting one massive anachronistic carryover from ancient Jewish idiomatic usage. But they are not. Rather, they express vital truths of the faith. And by linking God's name as his power and glory and as our knowledge of him to his name as symbols of sound produced by human lips they show us the way to direct access to this divine power and knowledge. The divine name itself is therefore the ultimate, the quintessential "sacrament," a real gift which has been offered by God and is accessible to all; through it every Christian has direct access to communion with God at every moment of his or her life.

Yet that is precisely what the imiabortsy denied. And in order to defend that denial they were forced not only to reinterpret but also to misquote texts whose authority they did not wish to question. A good example is what Troitskii did with one text from Fr. John of Kronstadt. To prove that Fr. John considered God's name to be "just another symbol" he quoted the following:

> Because of our bodily nature the Lord attaches, so to speak, his presence to some or other visible sign, he attaches his presence to the temple, to icons, to the cross, to the sign of the cross, ***to his name*** ... (qtd. in OIB 156; Troitskii's emphasis).

However, the text really reads:

> ... to some or other visible sign; for instance: in the sacrament of communion, he himself wholly settles into the body and blood; in repentance, he acts through the visible face of the priest; in

Name as Sacrament

baptism – through water; in the priesthood – through the bishop; in marriage – through the priest and the crowns He Himself crowns; in chrismation – through the oil; he attaches his presence to the temple ... (*Moia zhizn'*, 2:296)

Everything between "visible sign" and "he attaches" Troitskii omitted without even using an ellipsis to indicate its omission. Fr. Antonii comments: "Now, one wonders: was such a corruption done deliberately or not deliberately? Obviously deliberately, for the body and blood are not those signs and symbols with which Mr. Troitskii wants to number God's name." (OV 162) Troitskii had to drop those words because he was trying to prove a radical difference between "visible sign" or "symbol" and "sacrament." However that radical difference did not exist in the mind of Fr. John of Kronstadt, it did not exist in other saints of the church, and it does not exist in scripture.

There is much room for theological development here, particularly in the direction of showing how every act of Christian life can be in some respect an act of faith. All of life, every human action, can and should ultimately be a confession of God's name – and therefore truly a "sacrament" in the same sense in which we use the word to speak of acts like baptism and the eucharist. Fr. Antonii himself, however, did not go far beyond basic explanations aimed mainly at defending the faith from those who "not only rejected these truths themselves, but by force tried to make us agree with their delusions and repudiate the primordial faith of the Church in the name of the Lord." It was his consciousness of those truths and the attacks against them that:

> ... did compel us and until now does compel us to defend with all our strength the things we have learned by the mercy of the All-good God and by the teaching of the holy fathers – the divinity

and power of the name of the Lord – and to dare to step forward with a verbal defense of these truths, in spite of our admitted lack of skill in words and lack of expertise in theology. However, this consciousness compels us at the same time in no way to dare to present our deductions and conclusions as final and as inerrantly formulated church teaching. We only venture to present them to theologians more enlightened than we, only as certain "materials" for their further deductions and conclusions, hoping that the Lord will send defenders of the honor and power of his name more skillful than we, who will confirm our truth and correct our mistakes. (207-8)

Nevertheless Fr. Antonii's works, particularly *Apologiia* and *Opravdanie Very* are indeed foundational, and in the future any theologians who may wish to further explain the Orthodox Christian understanding of God's name will find in them an indispensable resource.

Sergius Bulgakov's Contribution

That work was to begin at the All-Russian Church Council which finally took place in 1917 and which established a special commission to discuss the matter of the Athonite monks "named imiabozhniki." Although this derogatory title was still used, the choice of people for the commission reflected a change in attitude on the part of church authorities by then: it was to be headed by Bp. Theofan, and Sergius Bulgakov was to present an in-depth report on the theological issues. Political events brought the council to a premature end and kept this special commission from completing its work, but given the people serving on it there can be little doubt that its conclusions would have been quite different from those set forth in the Holy Synod's decision of May 18, 1913.

Mr. Bulgakov did write the assigned report but was never able to present it. He was apparently disinclined to publish it himself, but it appeared posthumously in 1953 under the title *Philosophiia Imeni* (A Philosophy of Name). In general he takes in this book a position virtually identical to that of Fr. Antonii and the imiaslavtsy.

Bulgakov argues that God's names are not merely particular symbols of sound but are in fact every known quality of God:

> Every judgment is naming, and every judgment is – more precisely, potentially is – a name, can become one. Every predicate which we ascribe to Divinity is at the same time a naming of God: Provider, Creator, Good One, Eternal One, Blessed One, Holy One, etc. ... The ineffable, mystical, unknown, transcendent essence of God reveals itself to man in its characteristics; these characteristics are predicates to the divine Essence; and as predicates they, when they become subjects, so to speak, *pars pro toto*[60] become names of God – in the plural. (178-9)

So every revelation of God is a new divine name; man does not name God, but God names himself through man; the act of naming is in fact an act *of* God *in* man. And the imiabortsy are wrong in presuming that an "energy" can be separated from its "result" or "fruit":

> ... divine energy itself speaks about itself in man, reveals itself in word; and the word, the naming of God, becomes as it were its [i.e., the energy's] humanization, its human incarnation. "And the Word became flesh" here receives a wider interpretation: the incarnation of the Word occurs not only in the divine incarnation of the Lord Jesus Christ, but also in namings, which are

---

[60]"The part for the whole."

performed by man in answer to the action of God. Already by this alone the names of God cannot be viewed as purely human creations, as symbols (*klichki*) invented by man. To suppose that this is so simultaneously indicates not only a misunderstanding of the nature of the name, but also the greatest blasphemy. And to the highest degree characteristic is the helplessness with which the imiabortsy try to reconcile their psychological understanding of the nature of word and name with that reverence before the name of God to which the orthodox feeling of church reality, or at least outward correctness, compels them. (180-1)

Hence the forerunners of the modern imiabortsy are in fact the iconoclasts, and it is significant that the latter were actually called *onomatomakhoi*, the Greek equivalent of imiabortsy, by Patriarch Nicephorus (see 182).

The views of the modern imiabortsy carried to their logically inevitable conclusions can only result in pantheism (the very charge they leveled against the imiaslavtsy):

> And so the names of God are verbal icons of Divinity, the incarnation of divine energies, theophanies; they carry with themselves the seal of divine revelation. Here are united inseparably and unconfusedly, as in the icon, divine energy and human power of speech: the person speaks, he names, but that which he names is given to him and is revealed. It is this human side in naming which gives cause to skeptical imiaborchestvo to consider the name of God as a human creation, a label (*klichka*) or something like an algebraic sign (and in this sense "a symbol"). But in order to be consistent in this point of view, one must bring it to the end and acknowledge that also the content of word-naming is wholly a human affair, an act of human knowing, completely immanent to him [i.e., to the human]. Therefore, this will mean that God is completely immanent to the world and to man, in other words, that the world and man are god – the pathos of buddhism and

contemporary monism, [which are] hostile to Christianity with its faith in a transcendent Divinity who reveals itself. (186)

That the views of the imiabortsy are foreign to scripture is shown by their reinterpretations of it, of which they have no right:

> For every reverent or even simply attentive and well-intentioned reader of the Old Testament it must be clear that the expression "the name of God" occupies here a completely special independent place. To say that this is only a means for expressing the idea "God" means to say nothing, to manifest only a blasphemously light-minded attitude to the biblical text, reaching even to a direct distortion of it. ... And above all there are those striking instances where the expression "name of God" in no way can be interpreted simply as a synonym, a descriptive expression replacing "God," but designates a special means of God's presence, of the power of his name in his name. (194)

Even where "the name of God" does seem to be simply a "substitute" for or synonym of "God" one must ask why such turns of phrase were chosen:

> ... but here too this word usage by itself demands and presupposes an explanation: why did the genius of language (in the present case Hebrew) – and that through the divinely inspired writer – permit such a replacement? Why specifically does "name" became such a substitute? An adequate answer for this question exists in the foregoing discussions, but here we can only add that specifically this plentiful word usage ... in no way witnesses in favor of imiaborchestvo but completely to the contrary; it speaks about the meaningfulness of the name, of its weightiness, of its substantiality. (200)

All of this leads to the same practical conclusions made by Fr. Antonii concerning the name, or act of naming, as sacrament. Bulgakov too specifically compares it to the eucharist:

The religious lie (and not only misunderstanding) of imiaborchestvo consists in its "psychologism," in that here the effectiveness of God's name is connected exclusively with [one's] mood (*nastroenie*): let a person pray zealously and sincerely and he will feel the power of God's name, but in the reverse instance – no. The conditions for the reception of grace and the character of this reception, connected with the subjective moment, with the personal mood, they transfer to the objective meaning of what happens here. [They are] just like their Protestant forerunners, [who] denied in essence the sacrament of the eucharist by attributing to it only subjective meaning, according to which, in dependence on mood, one person communes, but another does not commune – as if whatever the mood might be it could supply an absent sacrament, replace its power. In the same way the power of God's name, they think, is communicated by the mood of the person praying, thanks to which the prayer will either be heard or not heard; as if one must especially persuade and call upon God to listen to man. However, God hears everyone who calls upon him, but not everyone who calls upon him turns to him with their heart and hears this hearing of God. And as the holy gifts are the body and blood of Christ identically for those who commune unto salvation, as for those who do so for judgment and condemnation, just so the name of God is the power of God, no matter how we approach it, reverently or blasphemously. To imagine that the gap between heaven and earth can be crossed just by human will is to inject psychologism, anthropomorphism, subjectivism, and finally – anthropotheism into the very heart of religion, into its holy of holies. (212)

Ultimately the issue is truly the very nature of prayer:

As it is impossible to be saved just by human power, so it is impossible to pray to God just by human power, if God were not inclined to this prayer even before we opened our mouths, if he were not present in it by his power, included within his name. ...

> Therefore in its essence prayer *is*[61] the invoked name of God. But as the name of God includes within itself divine energy, gives God's presence, then practically, energetically, one can also say, though with great imprecision, that the name of God is God. More precisely, in it is present God's power, which is inseparable from God's essence, and it is in this sense God himself. Every prayer is also a miracle, if one calls "miracle" a rupture in the immanent, the penetration of it by the transcendent – and this miracle is the name of God, which is Divinity. (212)

As for the formula "the name of God is God himself," even by its grammatical construction it does not imply the "imyabozhiye" at which the imiabortsy were so scandalized, insofar as predicate merely describes subject. The verb "is" is not like an algebraic equals sign designating absolute identity. Rather, these words express the divinity of God's name and ultimately its sacramental nature in prayer:

> ... this presence of Divinity in its name, which causes the reverent pray-er to exclaim, "The name of God is God himself," in no way introduces fetishism of the name, but reveals the eternal and incomprehensible sacrament of God's incarnation and condescension, the presence of God in his name, which is confirmed in the sacrament of prayer. (217)

Thus both Fr. Antonii Bulatovich and Sergius Bulgakov reached essentially the same conclusion: their defense of the real divinity of God's name was ultimately a defense of the reality of man's communion with God as a reality which takes place not just in certain specific rites fundamentally different from the rest of life, but in prayer itself, in all prayer. They were defending the foundational Christian belief that to every believer – ultimately

---

[61]Emphasis added to reflect implicit emphasis of "*i est*".

to every human being – is open the possibility of direct communion with God at each and every moment of life. This is precisely what Ilarion had meant, it is what John of Kronstadt had meant, and it is the fundamental truth of Christianity which is expressed in myriads of other ways throughout the Christian tradition.

Epilogue

After the Bolshevik revolution the Russian church found other things to be more pressing than theological quarrels, and little more was heard of this one, for several reasons. First of all, what began as private quarrels had escalated into churchwide controversy specifically because ecclesiastical authorities openly took stands, in the name of the whole Church, inconsistent with the Christian faith. But when the Moscow court dropped the requirement that imiaslavtsy repudiate in writing their faith in God's name in order to be received into communion with the church, those stands were effectively nullified, and so incentive for continued opposition to them was removed. Individual hierarchs did not abide by that decision, but this was a less pressing problem; false pronouncements made by individual bishops are everyday occurrences anyway and in any case are less harmful than falsehoods endorsed by the supreme authority of an autocephalous Orthodox Church. The latter situation calls for much more vigorous protest than the former.

In addition, the leading imiabortsy had one by one lost power or disappeared. The dissatisfaction in "higher circles" that had caused Abp. Antonii to be dropped from the Holy Synod eventually reached Abp. Nikon as well. Here the nature of the "higher circles" can be more clearly ascertained: Nivière quotes a 1915 letter in which the grand duchess Elizaveta Fedorovna suggests to the tsar that Nikon be dropped from the Holy Synod because "He has on his conscience his sin of Athos." (367) Nikon was dropped from the Synod in 1915. Little more is heard of him, and he died not long thereafter, at the Trinity-Sergius monastery near Moscow in December of 1918.

Until the revolution Troitskii kept up his anti-imiaslavtsy propaganda but afterwards fled, leaving polemics about the name of God behind him. He then taught for a while at the University of Belgrade, later at the Orthodox Seminary of St. Sergius in Paris, and later in the Soviet Union at the Moscow Theological Academy. He died in 1973.

Abp. Antonii, though dropped from the Holy Synod and demoted to the less important diocese of Khar'kov,[62] nevertheless remained quite powerful, and when the 1917 Council restored the office of patriarch he was among the three nominated to that office, from whom one was to be chosen by lots. But the lot fell to one of the other two, and not long after the revolution Abp. Antonii abandoned his diocese and became the leader of an independent church group calling itself the "Synod of the Russian Orthodox Church Outside of Russia." Ironically, of the Russian church and its offshoots, that group was the first to canonize Fr. John of Kronstadt and is so far the only one to canonize Tsar Nicholas II.

After the revolution Fr. Antonii Bulatovich returned to his mother's estate of Lutsykovka where he lived in a small cabin, stayed in his monastic garb, and served as a priest for the local parish. In December of 1919 he was found near his cabin by some of his parishioners, shot in the head. His Soviet biographer ascribes this act to robbers; this is possible but is perhaps less probable than the surmise of Fr. Antonii's sister:

---

[62]800 parishes vs. 1800 in Volynia; see Niviere 362. Ironically, the move made him Fr. Antonii Bulatovich's archbishop since the latter's family estate of Lutsykovka was not far from Khar'kov.

Epilogue

... he was a friend, a great friend, of the peasants. The peasants **liked** him **always**; both during the revolution and before the revolution and aft[er] ... and they said that when he had a service in the local church, the church was overfull. Perhaps this displeased the Bolsheviks, that he was ... that he had such a religious influence – and they destroyed him. ... They didn't arrest him. He was never arrested. ... Because he was extremely – how do you say? – democratic. In the real sense and best sense of this word. He was a democrat. He liked the soldier, he liked the simple heart, he said, "I like the simple people." He didn't like the sophisticated. He liked the ... plain ... truth. (Tape 4)

Revolutionary Russia was not a safe place for people who liked "plain truth." It is well known that the number of priests killed by the Bolsheviks reaches into five figures, so Mary Orbeliani's guess is not just a shot in the dark. In addition, it is hardly likely that robbers would go after a monk clothed in cassock and schema and living in a humble cabin, as these are the surest signs of poverty to be found in the Russian countryside. Finally, it is noteworthy that December of 1919 coincides with the advance of the Red Army towards Khar'kov (see Nivière 370). In any case, Fr. Antonii cannot have been less aware of the dangers inherent in staying to serve the spiritual needs of his local flock than were others in positions of spiritual responsibility who nevertheless fled to save their own necks; it would not be presumptuous to bestow on him the title of martyr for the faith.

As for the fate of Mt. Athos, although in May the Conference of London had endorsed the Russian project of turning over the peninsula to an international protectorate, the Conference of Bucharest in August of that year decided instead to recognize the Holy Mountain as annexed to Greece. That status has been maintained to the present day. How much the loss of a Russian majority affected this decision is difficult to say, but one thing is clear: the Russians' fear of what Greek sovereignty would mean for them had been quite justified. After the 1917 revolution the Greek government prohibited not only "repentant" imiaslavtsy but any Russian monks at all from settling on Athos, which policy it has maintained with rare exceptions up until the present day. And so the Russian population decline which began with the mass expulsions of July, 1913 accelerated and became irreversible. The Rossikon declined from its peak of nearly 2,000 monks to 560 in 1925, to 200 in 1940, and finally to about 24 which it has been able to maintain because a few monks have been allowed to move there relatively recently from the Soviet Union. The skete of St. Andrew's has been completely desolate for years. Both look like ghost towns, with many buildings standing only as shells of brick without roofs or interiors.

And so also the controversy over the name of God died. It was never again to trouble the Church of Russia, but outside of Russia it did feebly raise its head among Russian theologians in exile. Fr. Sergius Bulgakov (ordained in 1918) eventually developed a theological system around the idea of "Holy Wisdom" somewhat in the tradition of Vladimir Soloviev's sophiology, and in passing he equated God's name to "Sophia" as well as to God's "energy." (See *Svet Nevechernii* 210, 216) When in the 1930's the Moscow patriarchate condemned Bulgakov's sophiology, it said nothing about the question of God's name; but when Metropolitan Antonii Khrapovitsky's group also condemned his teaching, Bulgakov's support of the imiaslavtsy was lumped together with his sophiology and the two attacked together (see Sobolev). To say what degree the condemnations of Bulgakov's sophiology were justified is beyond the scope of this work, but a few observations are in order. The imiaslavtsy were protecting truths of the faith against those who would distort them; they were forced into that defense by their opponents, whereas "sophiology" was entirely an exercise in speculative theology, an attempt to work out a comprehensive theological-philosophical system. The two tasks are by no means to be equated. In addition, Bulgakov's system was built entirely around one word that, while certainly not insignificant, is nevertheless not exactly central to the biblical message. This cannot be said of the name of God, which occurs constantly throughout every level of the Christian tradition and is presented as the very cornerstone and foundation of the faith. "Wisdom," on the other hand, occurs relatively infrequently in scriptural, patristic, or liturgical texts, and one can reasonably doubt the wisdom of creating a theological-philosophical system around it. In any case, Bulgakov's teachings about God's name as expressed in *Philosophiia Imeni* are linked to his sophiology only by a few chance comments made after the fact. There is no justification for lumping the two together.

More recent references to the imiaslavtsy among Orthodox and non-Orthodox writers alike generally reflect a deplorable lack of true information due to the years when the most well-known publications printed only the slanders and misrepresentations of the imiabortsy. Typical is a popular book by the monk Lev Gillet about the Jesus prayer, in which he briefly mentions the imiaslavtsy and remarks that "Their theory was obviously inadmissible ..." while devoting his whole book to propounding the very same point of view they had defended. He even adopts their very phraseology when he says that "Jesus" is "the single word that is the Word himself." (72)[63] Others, including the Russian Orthodox theologian Fr. Georges Florovsky (see *Puti*,

---

[63]Another Orthodox theologian, Sergey Verhovskoy, similarly misrepresents the issues in the 1912-1917 controversy in an article written in 1948.

572), as well as most of the recent histories of the controversy, either do not discuss the theological issues or simply say they are unresolved. Some say that the Ecumenical Patriarch's condemnatory epistles "remain in force." But the Orthodox Church has no corollary to the Roman Catholic doctrine of papal infallibility. Others speak of the imiaslavtsy as a "religious movement." But Orthodox Christians do not speak of the eighth and ninth century defenders of the icons as initiators of an "iconodule movement."

Conclusion

If the cause of this complex theological controversy can be reduced to one basic issue, then that might be what is sometimes termed scholasticism. This approach to theology views it as a system of data culled from authoritative sources which can then be put into a comprehensive scientific system. Scholastic theology is characterized by a belief that these data can provide an answer for every question, that everything can be divided into neat and distinct categories for which there are always simple and clear rational explanations.

Into this system as it has existed and to some degree does exist in the Orthodox Church, a belief in God's name as a real "sacrament" simply will not fit. It cannot be reconciled with the view that would set aside seven and only seven "sacraments" as absolutely unique rites fundamentally different from other aspects of Christian life. It cannot be reconciled with the view that ascribes efficacy to "sacraments" only when they are performed by duly appointed hierarchs within the canonical limits of the Eastern Orthodox Church. And insofar as it presumes that every person has within himself or herself the capability of immediate and direct communion with God it cannot be reconciled with the view limiting the bounds of the Church to its official membership lists.

At the time of this controversy the scholastic approach to theology was widely accepted and taught in Orthodox theological institutions. That is why such a clash arose between the "educated" monks imbued with the rationalistic spirit of the late nineteenth century Russian seminaries and the "simple" monks imbued with the spirit of Bible, liturgy, and fathers – for the two "spirits" are at heart incompatible. That the imiaslavtsy were generally those who had never attended theological seminaries (including Fr. Antonii Bulatovich) reveals both the tremendous potential for evil inherent in such institutions and the tremendous power for good inherent in the liturgical life of the Church, its scripture, and the writings of its saints.

Scholasticism has been able to exist within Orthodoxy because on the surface it does not deny the essential truths of the faith. In Orthodoxy varying opinions can and do peacefully coexist; however, this is not because mutually contradictory beliefs are considered to be equally acceptable; rather, it is because of a recognition that people, including hierarchs, are fallible, and their making mistakes does not necessarily make them "heretics." However, when disagreements are perceived to be about essential truths of the faith, and especially when at least one side wants to force its view on the other, it becomes necessary to seek a definitive resolution to the question.

We have here an example of how that is done in the Orthodox Church, or at least how it was done in the Russian Orthodox Church of the early twentieth century. It is not a pretty picture. Major dogmatic pronouncements were influenced primarily by personal grudges, personal favoritism, intra- and inter-church politics, and interference from secular authorities. The supposedly conciliar mechanisms for assuring that such decisions reflected the mind of the Church were simply window-dressing for decisions predetermined by a few powerful individuals. Mechanisms for appeal served only to maintain an appearance of fairness while reliably rendering predetermined verdicts. Church leaders at every level from monastery abbots to Holy Synod acted as autocrats not responsible to anyone but themselves. And the way in which high positions of ecclesiastical authority could be occupied by people ready, willing, and able to use their power to perpetrate shocking cruelties on those with whom they disagreed is little short of mind-boggling.

It would not be true to assert that this is a highly unusual state of affairs, however. In fact, political, personal, and economic factors can be found to play important roles in nearly every major controversy that has ever rocked the church. Sometimes they seem to have been decisive. But in each such case it was the masses of simple church members, usually led by a few skillful apologists, who ultimately determined whether the victory of one side or the other would be temporary or permanent. Falsehood might appear to reign for years, even decades, but it was always ultimately doomed to fail so long as it did not capture the hearts of the masses of simple believers. So too in this controversy over the name of God. Had the imiaslavtsy been unable to prove that they were indeed faithful to the church's tradition, the "connections" through which earlier condemnations were reversed would have availed little. On the other hand, had the imiabortsy kept up their attacks, a more definitive resolution would have been necessary, and the heresy of "imiaborchestvo" would have been made famous by a definitive condemnation. But they did not and it was not. And seeing that it has not arisen again, it did not need to be.

As heresies go, "imiaborchestvo" is probably not to be classed with the worst. Just as the iconoclasts did, the imiabortsy could still profess belief in Jesus Christ as the promised Messiah who was crucified, died, was buried, and arose from the dead; and who was and is both fully God and fully man, one of the Holy Trinity. Even if their position carried to its logical conclusions would result in denials of even these basic truths, they did not necessarily sense the inner contradictions and did not themselves carry their beliefs to those ultimate conclusions. And in a sense they were not even as harmful as the iconoclasts, for they proposed no radical changes in the church's manner of worship.

Yet the denial of the divinity of God's name was the first step on a road that could only inevitably lead not to Christ but away from him, not to life but to death. And for the Russian Church to officially remain on record as endorsing such an inherently anti-Christian view would have caused incalculable harm to the Church in the following years. For that reason all Orthodox Christians owe a debt of gratitude to the work done by the imiaslavtsy in defense of the truth, particularly to those who accepted incredible hardships in defense of truths they themselves didn't even fully understand. Of them, Fr. Antonii Bulatovich played a role not unlike that of Maximus the Confessor in an earlier theological dispute. The issue there too was one seen by many to be about an obscure and unimportant point of theology. There too it seemed like only one dared raise his voice against the prevailing opinion of those in power, and that only he was endowed with the literary capability to do so. There too the defender of the faith died not in glory, not having been vindicated in his lifetime, but having seemingly been rejected by the Church he had so hoped to serve.

Both cases speak eloquently about the very nature of the Orthodox Church, as Bulgakov had suggested in 1913. Preservation of truth is not solely the responsibility of the church hierarchy – in fact, all too often truth has had to be defended *from* the hierarchy. That responsibility, in varying forms and degrees, belongs rather to each and every member. This is in turn possible because each and every member has personal knowledge of and communion with God himself through the indwelling Holy Spirit. And that is effected by the power of God's name –

in prayer, in certain rites like baptism and the eucharist, and in numberless other acts of faith which essentially constitute confessions of God's name.

These are indeed fundamental truths of the faith, not minor intricacies of esoteric theology. And all who are Orthodox are indebted not only to God for his work in preserving this truth within his church, but also to those people through whom he did it. If they made mistakes, so did all of the saints of the church, who were, after all, human. So it is in recognition of the debt of gratitude owed to them especially by all of us who are spiritual children of the Russian Church that I dedicate this work to the imiaslavtsy and particularly to Fr. Antonii Bulatovich. May God grant them "memory eternal" – an eternal name.

Bibliography

Aleksii, Hieromonk (Shepel'). *Bozhestvenno li imia "Iisus"?* Kiev.

Anatolii, Bishop. Letter. NV 1914 May 2:6.

Andronik, Hierodeacon (Trubachev). "Ukazatel' pechatnykh trudov sviashchennika Pavla Florenskogo." Bogoslovskie Trudy 23(1982): 280-309.

Antonii, Archbishop (Khrapovitskii). Letters. NV 1913 May 12:7. RI 1912 10:62-63; 15:60-62.

_____. "O novom lzheuchenii, obogotvoriaiushchem imena i ob 'apologii' Antoniia Bulatovicha." TsV 1913 20(May18):869-82. Reprinted in RI 1913 9:554-80 and SP 78-100.

Antonii, Hieromonk (Bulatovich). *Afonskii razgrom; Tserkovnoe bezsilie.* St. Petersburg, Dym Otechestva, 1913.

_____. *Apologiia Very vo imia Bozhie i vo imia Iisus.* Moscow: Religiozno-filosofskaya Biblioteka, 1913.

_____. *Hē doxa tou Theou einai ho Iēsous.* Thessaloniki, 1913. Reprinted in Papoulidis, *Hoi Rōsoi.*

_____. "Drevnye i novye uchiteli Tserkvi o Imeni Gospodnem." MO 1916 9-10(Sep-Oct):462-497.

_____. "Imia Bozhie v ponimanii i tolkovanii Sv. Grigoriia Nisskago i Simeona Novago Bogoslova." MO 1916 5-6(May-Jun):17-56.

_____. *Istina o istine k predotrasheniiu imeborstva.* Constantinople: Izd. Inokov Sviatoi Afonskoi Gory, ispovednikov Imeni Iisusa, 1912.

_____. *Istoriia Afonskoi Smuty.* Petrograd: Ispovednik, 1917.

_____. Letters. NV 1913 May 14:6; Jul 25:5; 1914 May 23:6. MV 1913 Mar 9:1.

_____. "Moia bor'ba s imiabortsami na sviatoi gore." IV 145(Sep 1916): 648-82; 146(Oct 1916): 133-69. Also published separately in book form (Petrograd, 1917).

_____. *Moia mysl' vo Khriste. O Deiatel'nosti (Energii) Bozhestva.* Petrograd: Izdanie "Ispovednik," 1914.

_____. *O molitve Iisusovoi.* St. Petersburg, 1912.

_____. *Novoe besoslovie imiabortsev.* 1912.

_____. *Opravdanie Very v nepobedimoe, npostizhimoe, bozhestvennoe imia Bozhie.* Petrograd: Izdanie "Ispovednik," 1917.

_____. "Ponimanie sviatym pisaniem imeni Gospodnia kak Bozhestvennago deistviia i Bozhestvennoi sily." MO 1916 7-8(Jul/Aug):261-297.

_____. "Ponimanie tserkov'iu imeni Bozhia kak Bozhestvennago Deistviia i Bozhestvennoi sily, svidetel'svuemoe iz molitv i vozglasov Bogosluzhenii." MO 1916 12(Dec):754-94.

_____. *Proshenie v Pravitel'stvuiushchii Sinod.* St. Petersburg, 1913.

_____. "Uchenie noveishikh uchitelei i pastyrei Tserkvi o Imeni Gospodnem i molitve Iisusovoi." MO 1916 11(Nov):613-40.

_____, ed. *Imiaslavie. Bogoslovskie materialy k dogmaticheskomu sporu ob imeni Bozhiim po dokumentam Imiaslavtsev*. St. Petersburg, 1914.

_____, ed. *Materialy k sporu o pochitanii imeni Bozhiia*. Moscow: Religiozno-Filosofskaia Biblioteka, 1913.

Arkad'ev, M. *Predrevoliutsionnyi russkii sram (Izgnanie s Afona podvizhnikov)*. Sremski Karlovtsi, 1913.

Askol'dov, S. "O Pustynnikakh Kavkaza." *Russkaia Mysl'* 1916 5(May):27-32.

Berdyaev, Nikolai. "Gasiteli Dukha." *Russkaia Molva* 1913 Aug No. 232.

"Blazhennaia konchina skhimonakha Ilariona, skhimnik, podvizavshisia v Kavkazkikh gorakh." Sergievskiye Listki / Feuillets de St. Serge 1936 1-2:12-14.

"Bozhieiu Milost'iu, Sviateishii Pravitel'stvuiushchii Vserossiiskii Sinod vsechestnym bratiiam, vo inochestve podvizaiushchimsia." TsV 1913 20(May 18):277-86. Reprinted in OIB VII-XVII, in MO 1913 6(June):322-29, in SD 18-28, in SP 39-49, and in MV 1913 May 31:1-2; Greek translation in EA 33(1913):187-92.

Bulatovich, Aleksandr Ksaver'evich. *Ot Entoto do reki Baro. Otchet o puteshestvii v iugo-zapadnyia oblasti Efiopskoi imperii*. St. Petersburg: Tipografiia B. Kirshbauma, 1897. Reprinted in the 1971 edition of *S Voiskami Menelika*.

———. *S Voiskami Menelika*. Moscow: "Nauka," 1971. Originally published in 1900. This edition also contains a 31 page biography of Bulatovich by I. S. Katsnelson.

———. *Tret'e puteshestvie po Efiopii*. A. B. Davidson, ed. Moscow: "Nauka," 1987.

Bulgakov, Sergei. "Afonskoe Delo." *Russkaia Mysl'* 1913 9(Sep):37-46.

———. *Dokladnaia Zapiska*. Paris: YMCA Press, 1936.

———. *Filosofiia imeni*. Paris: YMCA Press, 1953.

———. *Pravoslavie. Ocherki ucheniia pravoslavnoi tserkvi*. Paris: YMCA Press, 1965. French edition: *L'Orthodoxie*. Paris: Balzon, D'Allones & Cie., 1958.

———. "Smysl ucheniia sv. Grigoriia Nisskago ob imenakh." *Itogi Zhizni* 1914 No. 12-13, 15-21.

———. *Svet nevechernii. Sozertsaniia i umozreniia*. Sergiev Posad: Tip. I. Ivanova, 1917.

Chinnov, G. *Po povodu sovremennykh sporov ob imeni Bozhiiem*. Odessa: Sviato-Andreevskii Obshchezhitel'nyi skit, 1913.

Daubray, J. "Les onomatolâtres." *Echos d'Orient* 16(1913):455-56.

Denasii, Monakh. "Pis'mo avtora knigi 'Na gorakh Kavkaza' skhimonakha Ilariona na Afon k dukhovniku-ieroskhimonakhu o. N. Otvet na pismo o. Ilariona. Zakliucheniia i posledstviia." *RI* 1912 15:62-63.

"Ekklēsia Rōssias. Apofasis tēs Hagiotatēs Synodou tēs Rōssias peri tōn en Rōssia heuriskomenōn, teōs agioreitōn, monakhōn onomatotheitōn." EA 34(1914):119.

Engel'gardt, N. "Groziashchii Priznak." NV 1913 Apr 22:3.

"Epistolē Patriakhikē kai synodikē pros tēn hagiotatēn tēs Rōssias synodon kata tōn onomatotheitōn." EA 33(1913):44546. With Russian translation in OIB XXIV-XXVI; Russian translation only in SP 161-64; in TsV 1914 9(Mar 1):63-65; with comments in NV 1913 Feb 13:3; and in RI 1914 2:91-94.

Ern, V. "Spor ob Imeni Bozhiem (Pis'ma ob imeslavii). Pis'mo pervoe. Proiskhozhdenie spora." *Khristianskaia Mysl'* 1916 Sep:101-9.

_____. *Razbor poslaniia Sv. Sinoda ob imeni Bozhiem.* Moscow: Religiozno-Filosofskaia Biblioteka, 1917.

Filosofov, D. "Terkovnyia Dela." *Rech'. Ezhegodnik na 1914 god.* 284-307.

Florenskii Pavel. *Arkhiepiskop Nikon — rasprostranitel' "eresi."* Moscow, 1913. Co-author I. P. Scherbov. In *Materialy k sporu* 101-4. Ref. in Andronik, 287.

_____. "Ot redaktsii." Foreword to *Apologiia Very* by Antonii (Bulatovich). Ref. in Andronik, 288.

_____. *Stolp i Utverzhdenie Istiny.* 1914. Westmead, Farnborough, Hant., England: Gregg International Publishers Limited, 1970.

Florovsky, Georges. *Puti Russkago Bogosloviia*. Paris: "Svetlost'" 1937.

"Gde istinnyia prichiny besporiadok na Afone." *Strannik* 1913 10:419-23.

[Gillet, Lev.] *The Jesus Prayer*. Crestwood: SVS Press, 1987.

"Gnomodotēsis tou syllogou tōn theologōn kathēgetōn peri tēs eskhatōs emfanistheisēs en Hagioi Orei para tois rōssois monakhois kainofanous didaskalias peri tou onomatos Iēsous." EA 33(1913):123-25. Russian translation in OIB III-V; SP 33-36; and SD 12-15.

Grigorovich, Kh. "Imia Bozhie." MO 1913 2(Feb)203-14; 3(Mar):369-88.

Hamburg, Gary. "The Origins of 'Heresy' on Mount Athos: Ilarion's *Na Gorakh Kavkaza* (1907)." *Religion in Eastern Europe* 23(2003):2(April):16-47.

Hausherr, Irenee. *The Name of Jesus*. Translated by Charles Cummings. Kalamazoo: Cistercian Publications, Inc., 1978.

Heyer, Fr. "Fr. Antoniy Bulatovich, Russian Friend of the Christian people of Ethiopia." in *Transactions of Russian-American Scholars in the U.S.A.*. New York, 1979. XII:217-27.

"Hoi Iēsouanoi." EA 33(1913):145-46. Contains text of September 2, 1912 epistle of Patriarch Joachim III and April 5, 1913 epistle of Patr. German V; both are reprinted with Russian translation in OIB I-II, VI-VII. Russian translations: both in SD 3-4, 16-17 and SP 29,37-38; epistle of Patr. Joachim III in RI 1912 20:78-79 and Kliment 758; epistle of Patr. Germanos V in RI 645-47.

"Hoi onomatolatrai en hagiō orei." *Ekklēsiastikos Kēryx* 3(1913 Dec 15):708-20.

Ilarion, Bishop (Alfeev). *Sviashchennaia taina tserkvi: vvedenie v istoriiu i problematiku imiaslavskikh sporov.* 2 vols. St. Petersburg: Aleteiia, 2002.

Ilarion, Schema-monk. *Na Gorakh Kavkaza. Beseda dvukh startsev o vnutrennem edinenii s Gospodom nashikh serdets chrez molitvu Iisus Khristovu – ili – Dukhovnaia deiatel'nost' sovremennykh pustynnikov.* Batalpashinsk: 1907, 1910. Kiev Percherskaia Lavra: 1912.

Ioann, Skhi-Igumen. *Christ is in our Midst: Letters from a Russian monk.* Crestwood, N.Y.: SVS Press, 1980.

Ivol'gin, S. "Ob afonskom volnenii i dogmaticheskikh sporakh." NV 1913 Apr 11:4-5.

———. "Nasha Diplomatiia i Afon" NV. 1913 May 10:3-4.

Jesman, C. *The Russians in Ethiopia. An Essay in Futility.* London, 1958.

Kallinikos, Schema-monk. Letter. RI 17:61-63.

Katsnelson, I. S., and G. Terekhova. *Po neizvedannym zemliam Efiopii.* Moscow: "Nauka," 1975.

Khitrov, A. M, and O. L. Solomina, comps. *Zabytye stranitsy russkogo imiaslaviia. Sbornik dokumentov i publikatsii po afonskim sobytiiam 1910-1913 gg. i dvizheniiu imiaslaviia v 1910-1918 gg.* Palomnik, 2001.

Khrisanf, Monk. (Potap'ev). "Otzyv o stat'e Sviatogortsa 'O pochitanii imeni Bozhiia." RI 1912 17:54-61. Also in SP 17-23.

_____. "Po povodu stat'i Chernyi Bynt." IV 140(Jun 1915):718-19.

_____. "Retsenziia na sochinenie skhimonakha o. Ilariona, nazyvaemoe: 'Na gorakh Kavkaza.'" RI 1912 4:71-75; 5:57-59; 6:50-61. Also in SP 1-16.

Kievskaia Mysl'. 1914 Mar 8:3; Mar 27:5; May 1:4; May 9:5.

Kliment, Monk. "Imebozhnicheskii bunt ili plody uchenyia knigi 'Na Gorakh Kavkaza." IV 143(Mar 1916):752-85.

Komnēnos, Pantoleōn. "Hē en Hagioi Orei Thrēskeutikē eris." *Ekklēsiastikos Faros* 11(1913):361-372.

Kosvintsev, E. N. "Chernyi Bunt. Stranichki iz istorii Afonskoi smuty." IV 139(Jan, Feb 1915):139-160, 70-87.

Kusmartsev, Pavel. *Mysli otsev tserkvi o pochitanii imeni Bozhiiago. Materialy k vyiasneniiu Afonskago bogoslovskago spora.* St. Petersburg, 1913.

Lacombe, J. "Les moines onomatolâtres." *Echos d'Orient* 6(1913):555-56; 17(1914):265-66.

The London Times. 1913 June 19:7; Aug. 23:3.

Losskii, V. *Spor o Sofii.* "Dokladnaia Zapiska" prot. S. Bulgakova i smysl Ukaza Moskovskoi Patriarkhii. Paris, 1936.

Mandel'shtam, Osip. *Sobranie Sochinenii.* Ed. G. P. Struve and A. Filippov. New York: Izd. Imeni Chekhova, 1955. See No. 76, p. 75, "*I ponyne na Afone* ...".

Maevskii, V. "Epopeiia Bulatovicha." *Novoe Russkoe Slovo* 1972 Jul 14. Reprinted in *Istoricheskie Ocherki*, Buenos Aires, 1972.

Mel'gunov, S. "Sovremennye eretiki i sinod." RV 1913 Sep 4:3.

Mel'nikov, F. E. *V tenetakh eresei i prokliatii. K sovremennym sporam ob imenakh Bozhiikh.* Moscow, 1913.

Mikhail, Bishop. "Afonskaia Smuta." *Rech'* 1913 May 22:1; Jul 6:2.

_____. "Afonskaia Ugroza." *Rech'* 1913 Aug 12:2.

Moskovskiia Vedomosti. 1913 Mar 9:1; Apr 5:2; May 17:3; May 21:3; May 31:1-2; Jul 16:1; Jul 24:1; Jul 28:1; Aug 17:1; Aug 31:1-2; Sep 1:1; Sep 5:2; Sep 6:2; Sep 7:2; 1914 Mar 2:3; Apr 22:3; Apr 25:3; May 2:2; May 8:3-4.

"Nachalo dukhovnago suda nad imiabozhnikami." TsV 1914 11(Mar 15):598-99.

Nikon, Archbishop (Rozhdestvenskii). *Moi dnevniki.* 3rd ed. Sergiev Posad, 1914.

_____. "Moe dobroe slovo imeslavtsam." TsV 1914 41:1864.

_____. "Na opasnom puti." TsV 1914 17(Apr 26):788-794.

_____. "Plody velikago iskusheniia okolo imeni Bozhiia." TsV 1913 34(Aug 24):1504-21. Condensed version in MV 1913 Sep 5:2; Sep 6:2; Sep 7:2.

_____. "Velikoe iskushenie okolo sviateishago imeni Bozhiiago." TsV 1913 20(May 18):853-69. Also in SP 50-77.

Nivière, Antoine. *Le Mouvement Onomatodoxe: Une Querelle Theologique Parmi les Moines Russes du Mont-Athos (1907-1914)*. Unpublished doctoral dissertation. Université de Paris, 1987.

_____. "L'onomatodoxie -- une crise religieuse à la veille de la Révolution," in *Mille ans de christianisme russe, 988-1988. Actes du Colloque international de l'Université Paris X-Nanterre, 20-23 janvier 1988* (Paris: YMCA Press, 1989), 285-294.

Novoe Vremia (St. Petersburg). 1913 May 12:3; May 17:5; May 19:3; May 28:5; May 29:6; Jul 2:4; Jul 14:4; Jul 16:4; Jul 22:2; Jul 24:5; Jul 25:5; Jul 26:2; Jul 27:4; Jul 30:5; Jul 31:4; Aug 1:4; Aug 2:3; Aug 8:4; Aug 9:4; Aug 10:4; Aug 11:5; Aug 13:4; Aug 14:4; Aug 15:4; Aug 18:5; Aug 21:3; Aug 22:2; Aug 23:4; Aug 24:13; Aug 25:4; Aug 26:3; Aug 27:4; Aug 28:2; Aug 29:4; Aug 30:1; Sep 1:3; Sep 4:5; 1914 Feb 13:6; Mar 1:3; Apr 3:2; Apr 20:4,6; Apr 22:3,4; Apr 23:6; Apr 24:3; Apr 25:5; Apr 30:7; May 2:4; May 3:14,15; May 7:3,4; May 8:3.

O Sofii Premudrosti Bozhiei. Ukaz Moskovskoi Patriarkhii i dokladnyia zapiski prof. prot. Sergiia Bulgakova Mitropolitu Evlogiiu. Paris, 1935.

"Opredelenie Sviateishago Sinoda. Ot 27 avgusta 1913 goda za No. 7644 o peresmotre resheniia Sviateishago Sinoda otnositel'no imiabozhnikov." TsV 1913 35(Aug 31): 425-430. Reprinted in full in *Rech'* 1913 Aug 28:3-4; OIB XVIII-XXII; SD 30-41; SP 153-161; MV 1913 Aug 31:1-2; and RI 1913 17:1093-1100.

"Opredelenie Sviateishago Sinoda. Ot 14-18 fevralia 1914 goda za No. 1471, po povodu poslaniia Vselenskago patriarkha na imia Sviateishago Sinoda otnositel'no monakhov-imiabozhnikov." TsV 1914 9(Mar 1):61-63. Also in NV 1914 Mar 1:3.

"Opredelenie Sviateishago Sinoda. Ot 27 fevralia – 4 marta 1914 goda za No. 1676 po voprosu ob izdezhkakh na proezd predannykh sudu Moskovskoi i Sv. Sinoda Kontory monakhov-imiabozhnikov." TsV 1914 9:61-65.

Orbeliani, Mary. Tapes of interviews recorded by Richard Seltzer. Transcripts in the Appendix of "Heresy on Mt. Athos. Conflict over the Name of God among Russian Monks and Hierarchs, 1912-1914." M.Div. thesis, St. Vladimir's Orthodox Theological Seminary.

Pakhomii, Monk (Pavlovskii). *Istoriia Afonskoi smuty ili "Imiabozheskoi" eresi.* St. Petersburg: "Sodruzhestvo," 1914.

Papoulidis, Kontantinos K. "Anekdota engrafa peri tōn Rōsōn onomatolatrōn tou Hagiou Orous." *Makedonika* 1981 21:262-80.

———. *Hoi Rōsoi Onomatolatrai tou Hagiou Orous.* Thessaloniki: Institute for Balkan Studies, 1977. Also contains previously unpublished documents from Athonite *Iera Koinotes* and a reprint of Ieromonakh Antonii's book, Hē doxa tou Theou einai ho Iēsous.

Pederson, Johannes. *Israel. Its Life and Culture.* 2 vols. London: Oxford Univ. Press, 1964. See chapter entitled "Name," 1:245-59.

The Philokalia: The complete text compiled by St. Nikodimus of the Holy Mountain and St. Makarios of Corinth. 3 vols. Translated by G.E.H. Palmer, Philip Sherrard, and Kallistos Ware. Winchester, Mass.: Faber & Faber, 1986.

Polishchuk, E. S., ed. *Imiaslavie. Antologiia.* Moscow: Faktorial Press, 2002.

Pomekhin, Sava. "Afontsy-imiabozhniki." MO 1913 11(Nov):369-86.

Pravda o sobytiiakh, proisshedshikh v pervoe polugodie 1913 goda v panteleimonovom monastyre. Moscow: Izdanie Afonskago Russkago Panteleimonova Monastyria, 1913. Also in RI 1914 2:94-106 and SP 192-202.

Rech' [St. Petersburg]. 1913 Mar 19:4; Apr 2:2; May 17:4; Jun 7:3; Jun 14:1,3; Jul 13:4; Jul 18:2; Jul 21:3; Jul 26:2; Jul 27:4; Jul 30:3; Aug 10:2; Aug 21:3; Aug 22:4; Aug 24:4; Aug 25:3; Aug 28:3-4; Aug 29:4; Sep 1:4; Sep 3:4; Sep 12:3; Oct 10:2; Oct 12:5; Dec 1:4; 1914 Jan 11:4; Jan 18:6; Jan 23:3; Mar 8:5; Mar 29:4; Apr 16:3; Apr 17:3; Apr 25:?; Apr 29:4; Apr 30:6; May 8:3.

Russkii Inok (Pochaevskaia Lavra) 1912 19:57-59. Plus the following for which I have only seen entries in tables of contents: 1913 7:445-454; 9:582-84; 14:888-90; 15:958; 21:1321-35; 1914 1:48-50; 3:164-75; 4:214-28; 5:293-98, 312-13; 9:567-69; 10:612-24; 12:742-49; 13:823-838.

Russkiia Vedomosti (Moscow). 1913 Jul 2:2; Jul 9:4; Jul 14:3; Jul 18:2; Jul 21:3; Jul 23:3; Jul 24:1; Aug 10:2; Aug 22:3; Aug 23:2; Aug 25:3; Aug 28:3; 1914 Feb 16:2.

Sbornik dokumentov, otnosiashchikhsia k Afonskoi imiabozhnicheskoi smute. Petrograd: "Svet," 1916.

Schultze, B., S.J. "Der Streit um die Gottlichkeit des Namens Jesu in der russischen Theologie." Orientalia Christiana Periodica 17 (1951): 321-94.

Seltzer, Richard. *The Name of Hero.* Los Angeles: J. P. Tarcher, 1981. Historical fiction about Alexander Bulatovich's experiences in the Russo-Chinese war.

Senina, Tatiana. The status of divine revelation in the works of Hieromonk Anthony Bulatovich. *Scottish Journal of Theology* 64(2011):4:377-389.

Serafim, Archbishop (Sobolev). *Novoe uchenia o Sofii Premudrosti Bozhiei.* Sofia: "Rakhvira," 1935.

_____. *Protoierei S. N. Bulgakov kak tolkovatel'sviashchennago pisaniia.* Sofia, 1936.

_____. *Zashchita sofianskoi eresi protoiereem S. Bulgakovym pred litsom Arkhiereiskago Sobora Russkoi Zarubezhnoi Tserkvi.* Sofia: "Rakhvira," 1937.

Serafeim, Monk. *Kharismata kai Kharismatoukhoi.* Oropos Attikēs: Ekdoseis Ieras Monēs Paraklētou, 1987.

Sergiev, Ioann (Kronshtadtskii). *Moia zhizn' vo Khriste.* Moscow, 1894.

_____. *Mysli Khristianina.* 1903.

Slesinski, Robert. *Pavel Florensky A Metaphysics of Love.* Crestwood, N.Y.: SVS Press, 1984.

Smolitsch, Dr. Igor. "Le Mont Athos et la Russie." in *Le Millénaire du Mont Athos 963-1963 Études et Mélanges*. Vol. 1. Éditions de Chevotogne, 1963. 279-318.

Soborianin. "Afonskaia Raspria." TsOV 1913 29(July 25):1-3.

_____. "Likvidatsiia afonskoi istorii" TsOV 1913 42(Oct. 24):1-3. "Le sort de l'Athos." *Echos d'Orient* 17(1914):172-75.

Stolypin, A. "Imiabozhniki." NV 1914 Mar 6:4.

Sviashchennyi Sobor Pravoslavnoi Rossiiskoi Tserkvi. 9 + 2 volumes. Moscow, 1918.

Sviatoe Pravoslavie i imenobozhnicheskaia eres'. Khar'kov, 1913, 1916. (Editorship variously attributed to Abp. Antonii Khrapovitsky or Monk Kliment.)

Tikhon, Hieromonk. "Osobomu vnimaniiu inokov." RI 1912 4:69-71.

Troitskii, Sergei Viktorovich. "Afonskaia smyta." TsV 1913 20(May 18):882-909. Also in SP 101-48.

_____. *K istorii bor'by s Afonskoi smutoi (Otvet V. M. Skvortsovu)*. Petrograd, 1916.

_____. *Kak uchat ob imenakh Bozhiikh imiabozhniki i kak uchit o sem Sv. Tserkov'*. Odessa, 1914.

_____. Letter. NV 1914 May 3:15.

_____. *Novaia pozitsiia o. Antoniia Bulatovicha*. Also in SP 219-228.

_____. Novoe ispovedanie imiabozhnikov. St. Petersburg, 1915. Also in SP 239-257.

_____. "O. Ioann Sergiev (Kronshtadtskii) i imiabozhniki." TsV 1914 1(Jan 4):17-25; 2(Jan 11):67-78. Reprinted in OIB 152-71.

_____. *Ob imenakh Bozhiikh i imiabozhnikakh.* St. Petersburg: Sinodal'naia tipografiia, 1914.

_____. "Soobshcheniia is zagranitsy. Bor'ba s Afonskoi smutoi." TsV 1913 36(Sep 7):1636-43. Reprinted in OIB 172-79.

_____. "Uchenie afonskikh imiabozhnikov i ego razbor." MO 1914 2(Feb):226-43.

_____. "Uchenie Grigoriia Nisskago ob imenakh Bozhiikh." TsV 1913 37(Sep 14):1659-74; 38(Sep 21):1706-15; 39(Sep 28):1771-79; 40(Oct 5):1809-22; 41(Oct 12):1862-70; 42(Oct 19):1919-30; 43(Oct 26):1973-80; 44(Nov 2):2000-17; 45(Nov 9):2077-84; 46(Nov 16):2132-40; 47(Nov 23):2169-73; 48(Nov 30):2223-31; 49(Dec 6):2281-90; 50(Dec 14):2331-40; 51-52(Dec 21):2391-2407. Reprinted in OIB 1-151.

_____. "Zashchitniki imiabozhnikov." TsV 1914 5(Feb 1):268-81; 6(Feb 8):337-44; 7(Feb 15):393-98. First two parts reprinted in OIB 180-200.

Trubetskoi, E. N. "Svet Favorskii i preobrazhenie uma. *Russkaia Mysl'* 1914 5(May):25-54.

Tserkovno-Obshchestvennyi Vestnik. 1913 19:8-11; 1914 11:5-6.

Tserkovnyi Vestnik (St. Petersburg). 1913 11(Mar 14):346-47; 20(May 16):618-19; 21(May 23):640-41; 22(May 30):674; 24(Jun 13):747; 32(Aug 8):977-83; 33(Aug 15):1024; 39(Sep 26):1214-15; 42(Oct 17):1318; 46(Nov 14):1446-47; 48(Nov 28):1516-18; 1914 5(Jan 30):145; 19(May 7):559-60.

Van Ruijen, D. A. "Le 'Rossikon' ou monastère russe de St.Panteleimon au Mont-Athos." *Irenikon* 30(1957):44-59.

Vechevoi, I. "Afonskoe delo." *Novyi Zhurnal dlia Vsekh* 1914 April:44-51.

Verkhovskoi, Sergei. "Ob imeni Bozhiem." *Pravoslavnaia Mysl'* VI(1948):37-55.

Vykhodtsev, E. *Istoriia Afonskoi smuty*. Petrograd, 1917.

Ware, Archimandrite Kallistos. *The Power of the Name: The Jesus Prayer in Orthodox Spirituality*. Oxford: SLG Press, 1982.

The Way of a Pilgrim and The Pilgrim Continues His Way. Translated by R. M. French. San Francisco: Harper and Row, n.d.

Yakobson, S. "Russia and Africa." The Slavic Review 17,19(1939-40):623-37,158-74.

Zenkovsky, V. V. A History of Russian Philosophy. 2 Vols. New York: Columbia Univ. Press, 1953.

Zernov, Nicolas. The Russian Religious Renaissance of the Twentieth Century. Translated by George L. Kline. New York: Harper & Row, 1963.

www.ingramcontent.com/pod-product-compliance
Lightning Source LLC
Chambersburg PA
CBHW032249150426
43195CB00008BA/374